RIGHT THINKING
BILL HULL

NAVPRESS
A MINISTRY OF THE NAVIGATORS
P.O. Box 6000, Colorado Springs, CO 80934

The Navigators is an international, evangelical
Christian organization. Jesus Christ gave His
followers the Great Commission to go and
make disciples (Matthew 28:19). The aim of
The Navigators is to help fulfill that
commission by multiplying laborers for
Christ in every nation.

NavPress is the publishing ministry of The
Navigators. NavPress publications are tools
to help Christians grow. Although
publications alone cannot make disciples or
change lives, they can help believers learn
biblical discipleship and apply what they
learn to their lives and ministries.

CONTENTS

AUTHOR

Bill Hull is currently pastoring Green Valley Church in the San Diego area. Bill has been a pastor in the Evangelical Free Church for over ten years, serving congregations in Illinois and California.

He received a B.S. from Oral Roberts University and an M.Div. from Talbot Theological Seminary. Between college and seminary, he served on the staff of Campus Crusade for Christ.

Bill and his wife, Jane, have two sons, Bob and Kris.

Bill Hull is the author of *Jesus Christ, Disciplemaker*, a book published by NavPress.

Introduction

Fix your thoughts on Jesus.

Hebrews 3:1

Spiritual inertia is caused by many factors. But even more difficult and important than naming those factors is the challenge of finding a way out. It frustrates the soul to rely on a series of crises in order to go from one plateau to the next. How can we find a substantial basis not only for getting out of spiritual ruts but, once out, for learning how to stay out?

Here are three embryonic principles that form the basis of right thinking about spiritual growth. These three currents will be more fully developed throughout the course of this book.

✛ ✛ ✛

7

(1) *Right thinking begins in the mind.* The Apostle Paul put forth an intellectual challenge to all Christians:

> Do not conform any longer to the pattern of this world, but be transformed by the renewing of your mind. Then you will be able to test and approve what God's will is — his good, pleasing and perfect will. (Romans 12:2)

Transformation comes through the commitment of the mind. Without the proper knowledge and thinking we have no basis for personal change or growth. The mind is the pivotal starting place for change. Thus Paul repeatedly emphasized to believers the importance of mature thinking. "Brothers, stop thinking like children. In regard to evil be infants, but in your thinking be adults" (1 Corinthians 14:20).

✦ ✦ ✦

(2) *Spiritual maturity is not automatic; it is supernatural.* Some people believe that if we listen long and hard enough we will automatically change. But it's not quite that simple. We never automatically change for the better; God must be involved in the process. The difference between automatically changing and supernaturally changing is substantial. Paul compares biblical change to looking in a mirror:

> But we all, with unveiled face beholding as in a mirror the glory of the Lord, are being transformed into the same image from glory to glory, just as from the Lord, the Spirit. (2 Corinthians 3:18, NASB)

The Word of God is like a mirror that tells us the truth about ourselves. Only when we see the truth about ourselves are we willing to change. The key to personal change is Spirit-engendered insight that is based on Scripture.

When I look in the mirror each morning, I see the truth! This is similar to hearing the truth of Scripture. *Seeing* the truth, however, is not enough, for we do not automatically change in the presence of truth. As I stand before the mirror, I may recognize that certain adjustments are needed. But I must deliberately take the action to change.

Although positive change is not automatic, it is supernatural. True followers of Christ are indeed being transformed into His image from glory to glory, gradually closing the spirituality gap between themselves and Christ. But the source is *supernatural*—"from the Lord, the Spirit"—thus it is not automatic.

The first time I ice-skated I slid out onto the ice and promptly fell down. Each time I tried to get back on my feet I fell again. Finally I crawled to the railing and pulled myself to my feet. As I watched the other skaters, I noticed their joy and ease on the ice. Such joy was irresistible. With clenched jaw I ventured back out on that frozen danger and found that if one is willing to weather cold hands and a wet bottom, progress could be made. Whereas early in my attempts to skate I found the ice an unfamiliar, hazardous enemy, as I learned to accommodate to the ice it became possible for me to glide with an ease and speed that had been at first impossible.

Think of the ice as the Holy Spirit. By venturing out with the Spirit, I can experience personal progress in the Christian life. This growth does not come quickly or easily, for it requires learning a whole new way of acting and reacting. Real spiritual growth is a gradual process that takes place in a supernatural arena, often apart from our best human intentions. But the fruit of the Spirit progressively ripens as we move out with courage toward spiritual adulthood.

✛ ✛ ✛

(3) *Spiritual maturity is evidence of personal experience,* just as spiritual immaturity is evidence of a lack of experience. This principle is explained by the writer of Hebrews.

> We have much to say about this, but it is hard to explain because you are slow to learn. In fact, though by this time you ought to be teachers, you need someone to teach you the elementary truths of God's word all over again. You need milk, not solid food! Anyone who lives on milk, being still an infant, is not acquainted with the teaching about righteousness. But solid food is for the mature, who by constant use have trained themselves to distinguish good from evil. (Hebrews 5:11-14)

Let us focus on the statement revealing the root cause of immaturity: "Anyone who lives on milk, being still an infant, is not acquainted with the teaching about righteousness." What, then, is the root cause of spiritual immaturity? Where does it begin and how can it be corrected? Apparently the immature Christian is not "acquainted" with certain teaching. The word "acquainted" here means having experience. The Christian can hear God's Word, but unless he applies that Word it becomes merely an academic exercise. If spiritual babes are *without experience,* then the remedy is to *get experience.*

The mature, discerning believer is described as such in verse 14 because of "constant use," or practicing the right disciplines in life. We derive our word "gymnastics" from the Greek word for "trained" in this passage. An athlete must be dedicated in his training in preparation for competition. Paul uses the same root word in 1 Timothy 4:7 where he urges, "Train yourself to be godly." Just as an athlete dedicates himself for the contest, the Christian is to discipline himself for the goal of spiritual maturity.

This is the sign of progress from spiritual immaturity to spiritual adulthood: self-discipline in the right kind of experience. The cause of spiritual immaturity is lack of experience; the cure is to get experience. Each of us should ask, "Am I putting into practice what I hear? Am I translating theory into practice?"

Educators recognize that when people simply listen to a speaker they retain ten percent. If they hear a message, see it, and take notes, the retention level climbs to fifty percent. If they hear it, see it, take notes, and also do one related activity, the retention level jumps to ninety percent. If we Christians would simply put into practice what we learn, we would retain much more truth. It would be more than intellectual theory; it would be lived-out truth.

✚ ✚ ✚

In the heart of every believer is the desire for growth — a hunger to please God and serve Him. But how can you get from good intentions to success? How can you get unstuck, out of your rut, off the plateau? (1) Begin with the truth, which will transform your mind. (2) Realize that change is supernatural, not automatic, and that you must take the initiative. (3) Get the right kind of experience. This book examines concepts vital to the Christian life, and explains them in light of these three keys to spiritual growth . . . and in the light of Jesus.

I

RIGHT THINKING
ABOUT GOD

*To whom will you
compare God?*

Isaiah 40:18

During his long career as pastor of New York's Riverside Church, the late Harry Emerson Fosdick spent many hours counseling students from nearby Columbia University. One evening a distraught young man burst into his study and announced, "I have decided that I cannot and do not believe in God."

"All right," Dr. Fosdick replied. "But describe for me the God you don't believe in."

The student proceeded to sketch a rather strange and twisted caricature of God. When he finished, Dr. Fosdick said, "Well, we're in the same boat. I don't believe in that God either."

A.W. Tozer wrote in his excellent work *The Knowledge*

of the Holy, "Whatever comes into your mind when you think about God is the most important thing about you."[1] What we think about God determines our response to Him, and our response determines our behavior.

God is perceived as everything from an oppressive ogre to a benevolent old gentleman who will eventually allow everyone through the gates of heaven. Some philosophers argue that God, who is omnipotent, must also be cruel for allowing all the pain and evil in the world. Other philosophers conclude that God is loving and kind but also impotent, unable to do anything about the problem of evil. Concepts of God are as varied as the people who hold them.

To one degree or another we all have different gods. My concept of God may be radically different from yours. If you tell me your concept of God, I can roughly predict your spiritual future. To the extent that one's concept of God is out of step with Scripture, we can anticipate the degree of spiritual difficulty that will follow. Most people reading this book probably have an image of God that is biblically based. The Bible does give some basic information about the personality and nature of God.

In my opinion approximately fifty percent of what we believe about God is the skeletal image provided by Scripture. Much like a sculptor who begins his work with a wire skeleton, we begin our thinking about God with some basic biblical truths. The remainder of our concept of God is developed from other sources. Much of what we believe about God is based on relationships with authority figures, such as teachers, police, politicians, and especially parents.

Scripture teaches that God is our Father. Romans 8:14-17 speaks of a warm, loving relationship with a heavenly Father. Quite naturally, your ideas about a heavenly Father are colored by your relationship with your earthly father and with other father figures. If authority figures have related to you in harsh, judgmental ways, then you will have difficulty not thinking of God in a negative light. Then, when you fail, it will be difficult to accept God's forgiveness and release from guilt.

If I equate rejection with discipline because authority figures have disciplined me in harsh anger, then I will think God is rejecting me whenever I sin. Some children hear a continual voice from parents saying, "You'll never amount to anything." Then as adults they continue to hear that disparaging voice, making them feel continually worthless.

To the extent that our parental relationships were relatively positive and healthy, we have a high degree of ease in accepting the biblical concept of God. But until we gain a right concept of God, our spiritual pilgrimage remains dead in the water.

✦   ✦   ✦

Ask yourself the question, *"Is your God worthy of your love?"* If not, when trouble comes you will find it nearly impossible to trust Him. You will not be able to withstand the storms of life if your God isn't reliable. If He's not fit to love, then He's not fit to trust.

For an interesting case study in right thinking about the person of God, turn to the story of a Jewish woman named Hannah (1 Samuel 1:1-2:10). She demonstrated a trust in God amid great trial and pain. Hannah's God was not only fit to love but also fit to trust, for He stood up to one of life's greatest tests.

Year after year Elkanah went up from his town to worship and sacrifice to the Lord Almighty at Shiloh, where Hophni and Phinehas, the two sons of Eli, were priests of the Lord. Whenever the day came for Elkanah to sacrifice, he would give portions of the meat to his wife Peninnah and to all her sons and daughters. But to Hannah he gave a double portion because he loved her, and the Lord had closed her womb. (1 Samuel 1:3-5)

Polygamy was common in Jewish culture —not ideal, just common. There were some practical reasons. For one thing, it ensured in a world of high infant mortality that the family name would live on. Also, it provided for the care of women who otherwise would have been left destitute.

What is immediately clear is that Peninnah had children and Hannah did not. It seems likely that Elkanah married Peninnah for children and Hannah for love. Elkanah tried to compensate Hannah's childless grief by giving her a double portion for sacrifice.

Elkanah deeply loved Hannah, and Peninnah knew it. One can only imagine the tension in their home. Peninnah was the one blessed with children; Hannah was given extras to ease the pain. Peninnah's scorn became Hannah's pain: "And because the Lord had closed her womb, her rival kept provoking her in order to irritate her" (1:6).

The intensity of the Hebrew verb translated "provoked" indicates the forceful nature of this irritation. One can only imagine what Peninnah said—perhaps something like this: "You're not a real woman, Hannah, because your womb is closed." It was commonly held that a barren woman was being punished by God, that His favor was withdrawn. So perhaps Peninnah shrieked, "There must be some sin in your life, Hannah!"

How easy it is to believe this kind of indictment.

Such an attitude is common among Christians. I have counseled many people who believe that the difficulty they are experiencing must be the result of something they did wrong. But although I don't discount God's discipline, I see a great difference between God's loving discipline and the "judgment" these guilty, broken people feel. The key issue here is that a person with this kind of guilt complex has an inaccurate picture of God. The idea that God commonly gets angry with people, vindictively giving them cancer, striking them blind, or taking a child or mate, is a hideous deception caused by a lack of knowledge about the real God and by a negative exposure to authority figures.

Hannah gradually learned how to handle such an attack on her emotions and beliefs. But first she suffered much pain and humiliation. "This went on year after year. Whenever Hannah went up to the house of the Lord, her rival provoked her till she wept and would not eat" (1:7). The dam finally broke when Hannah just couldn't take the incessant pounding of Peninnah any longer. She sat at the table weeping, unable to eat. She just broke down.

Thanks to Elkanah, we have an example of how not to help a person through a difficult time. "Elkanah her husband would say to her, 'Hannah, why are you weeping? Why don't you eat? Why are you downhearted? Don't I mean more to you than ten sons?'" (1:8). In other words, the man was telling his wife that her sorrow was inappropriate, that *he* was enough compensation for her childless state. Elkanah was essentially saying to Hannah, *"Hey, Baby, who needs children when you have a guy like me? I'm enough for any woman. I'm worth ten sons!"* How typical of a man to overestimate his value and underestimate the emotional damage done to his wife.

During the months after the birth of our second

son, my wife experienced dark days of depression. On one occasion she was telling me that she was under the pile. It was her cry for help. On my way out the door, I shot back the comforting words, "If you're under the pile, then get out from under it!" Slam!

This type of callous insensitivity doesn't help. Elkanah's pompous attitude drove Hannah from the table. Can't you just picture this?

> Once when they had finished eating and drinking in Shiloh, Hannah stood up. Now Eli the priest was sitting on a chair by the doorpost of the Lord's temple. In bitterness of soul Hannah wept much and prayed to the Lord. And she made a vow, saying, "O Lord Almighty, if you will only look upon your servant's misery and remember me, and not forget your servant but give her a son, then I will give him to the Lord for all the days of his life, and no razor will ever be used on his head."
>
> As she kept on praying to the Lord, Eli observed her mouth. Hannah was praying in her heart, and her lips were moving but her voice was not heard. Eli thought she was drunk and said to her, "How long will you keep on getting drunk? Get rid of your wine." (1 Samuel 1:9-14)

Hannah flung herself down before God, and, crying out to Him, made a vow that if she was given a son she would dedicate him to the Lord. As much as this might seem like foxhole Christianity, it wasn't. For Hannah possessed a substantial track record of walking with God prior to this desperate prayer.

One must feel for Hannah. At first Elkanah misread what was happening, and then Eli missed the mark by thinking she was drunk. Hannah seemed to be the only one who understood what was going on inside herself.

"Not so, my lord," Hannah replied to Eli. "I am a woman who is deeply troubled. I have not been drinking wine or beer; I was pouring out my soul to the Lord" (1:15).

She didn't deny the pain; she didn't cover up. We often cover up our emotional turmoil to protect ourselves. When we are insecure in our relationships with others, we are afraid to tell them who we truly are. If we haven't experienced unconditional acceptance with others, we will do almost anything to avoid rejection.

When the emotional pressure is intense and we repress what is boiling inside, the pressure increases until explosion is the only option. If you have ever tried to sit on an inflated beach ball in the water, you know that it is a tricky maneuver. You can manage for a few seconds, but the inflated ball eventually wins out, popping up to the surface.

The same is true of emotional pain. It must be allowed to surface or else it will pop up in a more abnormal, uncontrollable form later. Delaying an emotional catharsis is a setup for potential tragedy. Pent-up emotions will eventually express themselves in negative terms—the man on a window ledge, the stomach full of pills, the final slamming of the door.

We hide emotional pain from others because we fear rejection and a loss of prestige in their eyes. But why would we repress our emotions with God? Often our prayer lives while we are in pain are both humorous and sad. We hide our troubled emotions from God and pray around how we really feel. We are angry with God. We don't like His program for our life at that moment, yet we tiptoe around the real issue. Our basic reason for going through this charade with God is the same as our reason for hiding our pain from each other. We are afraid that God will not accept us, forgive us, and continue to use us. We fear that somehow, once we tell God off, He will be so offended that the relationship with Him will be colored for life.

✛ ✛ ✛

E. Stanley Jones wrote, "What we know or think about God outside of Christ is wrong." What a marvelous statement; what a wonderful concept! When we fail spiritually or find ourselves in a situation much like that of Hannah, our key for knowing what God thinks is *Jesus*. Find from the Gospel record a case similar to yours. Then ask yourself, "What is God like?" Think Jesus. "What makes God angry?" Think Jesus!

The issue here is to know how Jesus would respond to our situation based on the Gospel record. This will give us a handle in order to deal with our emotions when going to God with pain. Jones said something else that I love: "If God isn't like Jesus, He ought to be." Jesus is so attractive, we fall in love with Him while reading the Gospels. Jesus, of course, is God. How Jesus responds is how God responds. There is no difference!

With many factors going against her, Hannah understood her own grief and was willing to express it. She "wept bitterly" (1:10), like a mama bear who has been robbed of her cubs. Hannah felt cheated, shortchanged. For her, life lacked total fulfillment without children. She was willing to do anything within the will of God to have them.

All the dynamics of depression, bitterness, and lifelong hostility were present. But what saved Hannah was her concept of God. Hannah was aware of a certain fact, of which Peninnah repeatedly reminded her: "The Lord had closed her womb." She knew that it was God who made her barren. But she didn't mistrust her God. Even in these difficult circumstances Hannah's God was fit to love.

This kind of trial will either drive a person to God or drive him away from God. The determining factor is one's concept of God. Hannah was driven to God, so she kept the lines of communication open. Throughout this account we are reminded several times that she kept praying, pouring out her heart to Him. When we are troubled, we pour out our insides only to those we trust and to those who accept us. Hannah recognized that God was compassionate and understanding, that He would accept her in damaged condition.

I have spoken with couples who have lost a child through disease or accidental death. Some of them turned from God saying, "No loving God could have allowed the suffering of our child." Others, while finding the loss just as painful, have come to grips with the loss and have deepened their walk with God. The difference is in what kind of God they had when they faced their trial.

People survive dark days and deepen their walk with God through trials only when they have it out with God. Hannah had it out with God. She poured out her heart, telling Him everything she felt, even the bitterness. She called on God to change the situation, to give her the child she wanted so much. Hannah didn't give up. She struck the best deal she could with her Lord. After venting her thoughts and emotions in the safe context of an understanding God, she changed.

Eli answered, "Go in peace, and may the God of Israel grant you what you have asked of him."
She said, "May your servant find favor in your eyes." Then she went her way and ate something, and her face was no longer downcast. (1 Samuel 1:17-18)

Hannah trusted God so much that after giving it her best shot she left it in His hands. After Eli blessed her, she left a freed woman. She cleaned up, ate some food, and wore a new expression on her face as she departed — the expression of a person at peace with her God and her circumstances. She must have been thinking, "My God is a loving, understanding, just God. He knows what is best. I've asked Him for a child. If He gives me one, I'll praise Him. But even if He doesn't, I'll still praise Him."

Unfortunately, many people in turmoil do not reach this point with God because they refuse to partake of an inner catharsis, a purging of their hearts to God followed by the release of tension and frustration that builds up inside. If we want to experience this kind of inner cleansing, we need to make our prayers like Hannah's prayers: honest, fervent, and aggressive in petitions.

Hannah returned home with a renewed confidence that, regardless of the outcome, God's will would be accomplished. It is liberating to be at peace with the will of God, to know you have fulfilled your responsibility by voicing your opinion and submitting your requests. The results, then, are left with God, who loves you and desires the very best for you. That's the kind of relationship you and God can live with.

✦ ✦ ✦

God has proven generous again and again in my life. He not only meets my needs but also gives me many additional blessings because I am His child. He is pleased to lavish good things on all His children. For this reason Hannah was at peace with her requests and her circumstances.

Scripture indicates God's interest in Hannah with the short statement, "The Lord remembered her" (1:19).

Hannah was with child, filled with the joy and wonder of the Lord. I don't believe her attitude would have been different even if the Lord had said no. She probably would have swallowed hard and kept trusting her good God, believing it best for her and the family that she have no child. She didn't have to *like* it—just *accept* it.

The trusting was not over. The first struggle over being barren was difficult, but keeping the commitment to give her son to the Lord no doubt proved to be agonizing. We find the story in 1 Samuel:

> When the man Elkanah went up with all his family to offer the annual sacrifice to the Lord and to fulfill his vow, Hannah did not go. She said to her husband, "After the boy is weaned, I will take him and present him before the Lord, and he will live there always."
>
> "Do what seems best to you," Elkanah her husband told her. "Stay here until you have weaned him; only may the Lord make good his word." So the woman stayed at home and nursed her son until she had weaned him.
> (1 Samuel 1:21-23)

At three years of age the weaning process was basically completed. What if you had only three years with your child, and knew it in advance? Only three years to instill important values and learning! Hannah, I'm sure, wanted to make every moment count. It would be not only a time to cherish but also a time of pain. For there would be occasions such as taking the boy to the temple for religious festivities, reminding Hannah of the day when she would eventually have to give him up.

This story serves to remind us of the importance of shaping a young mind in the early years of life. There are several issues that parents must note and practice if the early years are to count. First, parents must be aware of how influential their modeling is. The love of parents for each other is the greatest single teaching tool parents possess. It breeds confidence and security in a child to know that his mom and dad are a team, that they are committed to each other and committed to him. This kind of commitment communicates on an emotional level. Kids see it and feel it.

I recently heard a radio report about the results of negative parental modeling in abusive families. A woman and her three-year-old son found protection in a shelter for battered women. The first day the three-year-old began bashing a little girl's head into the coffee table. After the workers separated the two children, the boy's mother began to cry, saying, "That's exactly what my husband was doing to me last night." Such is the power of modeling.

We erroneously believe that the impression we leave on the young is like a sculptor who carefully models his clay into exactly the form desired. Actually, the impression we leave is more like a man running along a path who stumbles and falls headlong into a pile of clay. The impression we leave is the reality of who we are.

It is vitally important to impress on a child a sense of belonging and a knowledge that he is loved and special. Positive time spent with a child communicates a sense of worth. Furthermore, a sense of purpose is needed. A child needs to know that God has a plan for his life. He needs to be sure that if he walks with God, God can be trusted to give him His best. When a child has no sense of belonging, of being loved, of having a God-oriented purpose, then he is vulnerable to insecurity, anxiety, confusion, and poor self-esteem.

Elkanah and Hannah tried to squeeze a lifetime of training into three years. Hannah must have felt great

love for Samuel, who was a gift from the Lord, a special
child. How could she ever give him up? Her inner turmoil
must have been profound.

If you have witnessed a mother nursing her baby,
you can see there is a special bond that words fail to
capture. What parent hasn't tiptoed into a child's room
just to watch him sleep? Jane and I still like to sit up
late and giggle over our kids' baby pictures. Parents can
become rather misty and nostalgic remembering the first
steps and the first "Ma-ma" and "Da-da" uttered. After
experiencing all these priceless joys, giving up your
three-year-old, even for full-time service to the Lord, would
be a great challenge.

Imagine Hannah leaving home on that fateful day,
the day she was to dedicate Samuel to the Lord and leave
him at Shiloh.

> After he was weaned, she took the boy with her, young
> as he was, along with a three-year-old bull, an ephah of
> flour and a skin of wine, and brought him to the house
> of the Lord at Shiloh. When they had slaughtered the
> bull, they brought the boy to Eli, and she said to him,
> "As surely as you live, my lord, I am the woman who
> stood here beside you praying to the Lord. I prayed for
> this child, and the Lord has granted me what I asked
> of him. So now I give him to the Lord. For his whole
> life he will be given over to the Lord." And he worshiped
> the Lord there. (1 Samuel 1:24-28)

As Hannah stood before Eli, those magnificent words
of trust came from her mouth. It was difficult enough
for Hannah to give up her son, but there was a certain
factor that made it especially difficult.

Hophni and Phinehas, Eli's boys, were notorious

brats as children and unprincipled exploiters as priests.
Eli was a lousy father, a fact that is documented in the
book of 1 Samuel. Not only was he a bad father, but
everyone in Israel knew it, including Hannah! Can you
imagine turning over your most precious child to a man
who botched it with his own children? How could Hannah
possibly do it? The answer is that her concept of God
allowed her to trust Him with anything, even her miracle
child.

Although giving up her child was deeply painful,
Hannah found in her relationship to God the confidence to
go on praising Him. Her prayer, recorded in 1 Samuel 2,
is a marvel.

> My heart rejoices in the Lord;
>> in the Lord my horn is lifted high.
> My mouth boasts over my enemies,
>> for I delight in your deliverance.

> There is no one holy like the Lord;
>> there is no one besides you;
>> there is no Rock like our God.

> Do not keep talking so proudly
>> or let your mouth speak such arrogance,
> for the Lord is a God who knows,
>> and by him deeds are weighed.

> The bows of the warriors are broken,
>> but those who stumbled are armed with strength.
> Those who were full hire themselves out for food,
>> but those who were hungry hunger no more.
> She who was barren has borne seven children,
>> but she who has had many sons pines away.

The Lord brings death and makes alive;
    he brings down to the grave and
      raises up.
The Lord sends poverty and wealth;
    he humbles and he exalts.
He raises the poor from the dust
    and lifts the needy from the ash heap;
he seats them with princes
    and has them inherit a throne of honor.

For the foundations of the earth are the Lord's;
    upon them he has set the world.
He will guard the feet of his saints,
    but the wicked will be silenced in darkness.

It is not by strength that one prevails;
    those who oppose the Lord will be shattered.
He will thunder against them from heaven;
the Lord will judge the ends of the earth.

He will give strength to his king
    and exalt the horn of his anointed.

(1 Samuel 2:1-10)

Hannah was rejoicing that God allowed her to give life to this special young man. She trusted her God completely. As she walked home that day it was with thanksgiving in her heart.

Hannah's story forces our concept of God to the wall. Is our God fit to love? Can our God be trusted with the most precious of possessions? Is our God Hannah's devil?

As human beings made in the image of God, we need to look at the God-human Jesus in order to best understand God. *Whatever you think about God outside of*

Jesus is wrong. When your circumstances challenge the goodness and compassion of your God, think Jesus.

NOTES: 1. A.W. Tozer, *Knowledge of the Holy* (New York: Harper and Row, 1961), page 9.

II

RIGHT THINKING ABOUT OBEDIENCE

*The great and awesome God
keeps his covenant of love with
those who love him and
obey his commands.*

Nehemiah 1:5

Love and obedience are strange bedfellows, rarely thought of as companions. If someone asked my children, "Do you love your parents?" they would reply, "Yes." If that person followed the first question with, "Do you obey your parents?" their answer might not be affirmative. This I know for sure: They would not immediately see a direct relation between love and obedience.

The Apostle John never allowed love to dissolve into a simple emotion. His writings are excruciatingly practical. In his first Epistle, John examined the authenticity of Christian love in practical terms. *Do you love the brethren? Are you meeting the needs of your brothers? Are you willing to sacrifice for your Christian friends?* John made love something one can taste, touch, see, and measure.

Jesus said, "If you love me, you will obey what I command" (John 14:15). If we are not keeping Jesus' commandments, the sobering truth is that, according to His criteria, we do not love Him! We may feel warm about God. We may enjoy singing His praises, hanging around His people, and reading His Book. But without obedience we are not really loving God! Love for God develops steadily as we grow in our obedient service to Christ.

Love without commandment-keeping is not love, and obedience for any other reason than love is legalism. *Agapē* love is willful obedience that leads to commandment-keeping. It is both an attitude and an action. Love expresses itself in obedience; true love requires both the attitude and the action, both emotion and expression of that emotion in concrete terms. The only way we can prove to ourselves and to God that we love Him is through obedience.

We need to understand what actually triggers love — the kind of love that leads to obedience, which leads to a life of power and meaning. Once again John explains: "We love because he first loved us" (1 John 4:19). God expressed His love in action in a historical context. Otherwise, mankind would never have been the wiser to the extent of God's interest. Without knowing of God's caring act of sending His Son, we would be unaware of His love for us.

When my wife and I first met, we were attracted to each other but we were not in love. As our relationship developed, we began to sense attributes in each other that were worthy of more than mere admiration. One of her first signs of deepening interest was her act of making me a pumpkin pie because she knew it was my favorite. This was followed by other small but symbolic acts of love. If she had done nothing, even though verbally expressing love, then her love for me would have remained in question.

Paul expressed this persuasive nature of love in action when he wrote, "For Christ's love compels us" (2 Corinthians 5:14). There is indeed an irresistible force to God's love. Because Paul was overwhelmed with the action that God had taken in His Son, he found it easy to love God back. Loving obedience means keeping His commandments regardless of our emotions and regardless of our circumstances. Though most of the time the emotions will be there, we should love Him back even when we don't feel like it. We should desire, as did Paul, to love God in response to His love for us in Christ.

✛   ✛   ✛

Jesus emphasized that loving obedience brings about a release of the immense potential within each believer. He promised two major benefits to the obedient believer. The first is the help of another Teacher and Guide. Jesus said, "And I will ask the Father, and He will give you another Helper, that He may be with you forever" (John 14:16, NASB).

This statement indicates that if you love Jesus you will keep His commandments (verse 15), thus leading Him to take action to help you. He will ask the Father to help you by sending a Helper who will be with you forever. The word translated "Helper" is a combination of two Greek words: *para*, meaning "alongside," and *kaleō*, meaning *"to call."* The Helper, then, is One who is called alongside to help. Some have translated this word "Comforter" or "Strengthener." The Helper's work is to encourage, comfort, exhort, and serve as an advocate.

A continuation to verse 17 helps at this point: "[He is] the Spirit of truth. The world cannot accept him, because it neither sees him nor knows him. But you know him, for he lives with you and will be in you."

The identification of the Helper as the Spirit of truth indirectly indicates the deity of the Spirit. Jesus stated, "I am the truth" (John 14:6), and then proceeded to call the Helper the Spirit of truth.

Jesus was preparing His disciples for His death, giving them hope for the dark days ahead. He reassured them, "I will not leave you as orphans; I will come to you" (14:18). He would not leave them alone, helpless, without resource. Coming to them does not refer to Jesus' Second Coming, for He said, "Before long, the world will not see me anymore, but you will see me. Because I live, you also will live." Because He was alive, they would experience the life of God in them. The vitality of their spiritual lives would then authenticate His being alive.

The Helper made a new relationship possible, an intimate kind of union never before known. Jesus said, "On that day you will realize that I am in my Father, and you are in me, and I am in you" (John 14:20). The disciples were to experience not the pain of separation but rather the benefits of an even closer relationship with God.

The life of God is intricately interwoven with the Godhead and the believer. Jesus told His disciples that He was leaving (verse 12), but that His departure would greatly enhance their ministry. They would receive the Spirit, but the world would not; they would see Him, but the world would not; they would know Him, but the world would not. In that day they would see things that they had never seen before.

When I look up on a clear night, I see many anonymous,

sparkling lights. But when an astronomer looks, he sees a great deal of interesting and meaningful formations of planets, stars, and galaxies. When I look at a forest, I see trees, bugs, and a few frightened animals. What a naturalist sees in a forest is a beautiful and complex world that can occupy his entire lifetime in study. When my wife watches a basketball game, she notices the obvious: men in shorts running up and down a court trying to score baskets. I see the 1-3-1 full-court press, a pick-and-roll, a give-and-go, the back-door, and the beauty of the fast-break.

The world looks at the Church and many thoughts are conjured up in their minds. What they don't see is what the Spirit-filled believer sees: a Body, a family, a building made without hands, an army preparing to march into the world with the message of Christ. The Church is a beautiful mosaic of humanity fused together by God's marvelous grace. It's His number-one project.

+ + +

Obedient Christians experience the fullness of the Holy Spirit. Calvin said that true knowledge of God is born out of obedience. Case in point: Peter cowered in the presence of a slave girl, denying that he even knew Jesus, but at Pentecost he preached powerfully to thousands. Think of the frightened disciples who scattered and ran for their lives when Jesus was arrested. Yet after Pentecost they exhibited a willingness to face lions and endure torture. Some were pulled apart on the rack; others were bound in skin bags and thrown into the sea; still others served as living torches, or were mangled and mashed. They endured horrid torture rather than denying Jesus.

The power of the Spirit transforms us from fearful

followers to obedient disciples. Obedience demonstrates how a Christian feels toward God. There are special benefits for such a person. An obedient Christian is loved by the Father and in turn loved by Jesus. This benefit of obedience gives rise to an important question: Does God's love for me depend on my obedience?

We love because he first loved us. (1 John 4:19)

Hope does not disappoint us, because God has poured out his love into our hearts by the Holy Spirit, whom he has given us. (Romans 5:5)

God demonstrates his own love for us in this: While we were still sinners, Christ died for us. (Romans 5:8)

These verses teach that God took the initiative—He first loved us. Why He loves us in our fallen condition is one of life's great mysteries. Even so, the fact is present that God first loved us and sent His Son to rescue us from our plight.

Jesus challenges us to a deeper love, a growing love that is found only in relationship. Sadly enough, many Christians' relationship with God stops just a little beyond the point of responding in faith to His first love for us. They receive Christ, but fail to grow into a mature relationship.

God initiates His love toward us in His Son. This *initiating love* sets a whole love process in motion:

1. He initiates His love toward me.
2. I respond in love to His love through my obedience.
3. He returns my love by loving me back again.

With God we experience the reciprocal give-and-take of a true loving relationship. He loves me; I love Him back in my obedience; He then returns His love in specific ways that meet my needs. Ideally, God and the Christian are constantly progressing in the level of their love for each other.

Regarding the obedient Christian, Jesus promised, "I . . . will love him and show myself to him" (John 14:21). This process is real and concrete: God reveals Himself to us by helping us overcome a problem, complete a project, or get through a difficult time. Down the path of obedience we find the hidden details of God's plan for our lives, with specific knowledge of how God works. The obedient life is an endless treasure hunt, a search for the deeper things of God.

Many times I have heard others say or thought to myself, "I wish I knew God's will for me." "I don't seem to understand God's will on this matter." "I don't sense God's presence." This lack of discernment abounds among Christians. That's why conference workshops on knowing God's will are usually crammed with inquisitive alumni of other similar sessions. They are frustrated from a lack of direction.

But until we Christians admit that the reason we are fuzzy on God's will is our own disobedience, we will make no progress. We have unmet needs in our lives because of a failure to obey God. Because of unmet needs in our individual lives, the rash of unmet needs in the Church is at an epidemic level.

God has asked us to become disciples, to be established in the Word, prayer, fellowship, and witnessing. He has asked us to live a holy life and to give Him first place in our time, talent, and treasure. Until we decide that we will love God by obeying Him, *nothing will change!* God will not guide a stationary object. He doesn't need to; it's not going anywhere. Many are looking for a way to wire around obedience—a shortcut, an escape hatch from reality.

It is aggravating to observe Christians looking for the easy way out of their responsibility to obey God. They hope that a song, a sermon, a friend, a Christian superstar, or a secret "zap" from on high will solve the dilemma of the Christian life for them. The person who lives the Christian life in such an erratic way usually becomes a religion addict, constantly looking for a spiritual fix or some instant supernatural stimulation. The spiritual highs from musical concerts or other greatly emotional experiences eventually wear off, leaving the person more desperate than ever for something more.

G.K. Chesterton said, "There is nothing so weak for lasting results as this enormous importance attached to immediate victory. . . . There is nothing that fails like success."[1] Spiritual panaceas and quick-fixes give only temporary relief. They fail because they leave out the deeper dimensions of the Spirit. Each of us has a personal need for lasting character, maturity, patience, endurance, and the mastering of scriptural fundamentals that will make it possible for a long, healthy Christian experience. Shortcuts simply don't work. I don't like them because every time I take one I have to start over again.

There is no substitute for obedience. God offers no alternative. The person who knows God's will is the obedient believer. God promises the obedient believer that the details of His plan will be found on the path of obedience.

Jesus said, "He who does not love me will not obey my teaching. These words you hear are not my own; they belong to the Father who sent me" (John 14:24). If obedience isn't present, then love isn't present. On the other hand, love leads to obedience, which leads to power and guidance of the Spirit, which gives rise to an ever deepening walk with the Lord. Deep within every Christian there is the desire to have God as a close friend. It is the factory equipment that comes with regeneration.

There is a particular question that confronted Jesus' disciples, who were to carry on after His departure. It is the same question that every Christian must ask: "Do I love Jesus?" If I do love Him, my obedience will prove it. If I am disobedient, Jesus says that, regardless of my word, I don't really love Him.

How does a person get started in the active pursuit of loving Jesus? R.A. Torrey tells a story that helps put this matter in perspective:

A little girl came to the great English preacher, Mark Guy Pearse, one day and, looking up into his face quite wistfully, said, "Mr. Pearse, I don't love Jesus. I wish I did love Jesus, but I don't love Jesus. Won't you please tell me how to love Jesus?"

The preacher looked down into those eager eyes and said to her, "Little girl, as you go home today keep saying to yourself, 'Jesus loves me. Jesus loves me.' And when you come back next Sunday I think you will be able to say, 'I love Jesus.'"

The next Sunday the little girl came up to him again, this time with happy eyes and a radiant face, and exclaimed, "Oh, Mr. Pearse, I do love Jesus, I do love Jesus. Last Sunday as I went home I kept saying to myself, 'Jesus loves me. Jesus loves me.' And I began to think about His love and I began to think how He died upon the cross in my place, and I found my cold heart growing warm, and the first I knew it was full of love for Jesus."[2]

The best way to embark upon a love for Jesus is to put your love in action. First, get into the Word and meditate on His love and what He has done for you. Second, check out His commandments to see what you are called to obey. Third, lovingly step out in obedience, regardless of feelings and emotions. Finally, allow God to lead you as you walk down the path of obedience, enjoying the adventure of discovering spiritual treasures.

Friedrich Nietzsche wrote, "The essential thing in heaven and earth is that there should be long obedience in the same direction; there thereby results, and has always resulted in the long run, something which has made life worth living."[3] Jesus taught that life is worthwhile and that we accomplish our mission only when we learn to obey Him regardless of emotions or circumstances.

NOTES: 1. Eugene Peterson, *Traveling Light* (Downers Grove, IL: InterVarsity Press, 1982), page 96.
2. R.A. Torrey, *The Power of Prayer and the Prayer of Power* (Grand Rapids, MI: Zondervan, 1924), pages 131-132.
3. Friedrich Nietzsche, *Beyond Good and Evil*.

III

RIGHT THINKING
ABOUT THE
SPIRIT-FILLED LIFE

The Spirit of God has made me;
the breath of the Almighty
gives me life.

Job 33:4

People are attracted to power. Whether it is the heady experience of high political office, leadership in a church, or popularity in the neighborhood gang, power intrigues us. We are captured by the wonder of jet aircraft, the awesome destructive potential of nuclear weapons, and the beauty and grace of the Olympic athlete.

People of the world are not the only ones interested in power. Christians have also demonstrated a desire for power ever since the inception of the Church. The emphasis on power can be clearly seen by a casual reading of the Acts of the Apostles. The early Church had the world on the edge of its seat because of the signs, wonders, and miracles seasoning the lives of early Christian leaders.

Subsequent Christian luminaries have likewise spoken of power. John Wesley, recalling his conversion, spoke of being strangely warmed. And when asked why so many people came to hear him preach, Wesley replied, "I just set myself on fire and people come to watch me burn." D.L. Moody, Charles Finney, R.A. Torrey, and others spoke of a sense of great spiritual power during their ministries.

As a college student, I came to Christ in a white-hot spiritual atmosphere where people just expected to experience God's power. People from the four corners of the United States would come to our campus expecting to be touched by the power of God. I can recall spending hours in the woods behind the campus crying out to God for more power.

As I matured in Christ I came to realize that there was great confusion in the body of Christ concerning the power of God. Some people claimed that the key to power was a holy life, others said prayer, some spoke of the baptism of the Holy Spirit, while others said it was knowledge of the Word. One thing was clear: Regardless of the precise formula, the power of God is linked to the Spirit of God. The Bible speaks about the fruit of the Spirit, being filled with the Spirit, walking in the Spirit, and being baptized in the Spirit. One certainty of Scripture is that anything supernatural has to come from God via His Spirit.

✦ ✦ ✦

What does it mean to be *filled* with the Spirit? Ephesians 5:18 is the only New Testament command for us to be filled with or controlled by the Spirit: "Do not get drunk on wine, which leads to debauchery. Instead, be filled with the Spirit." The common denominator between the two imperatives "Do not get drunk" and "Be filled" is one of influence. To be drunk is to be under the control of a foreign substance that alters your behavior. To be filled with the Spirit is to be under the control of the Spirit, who alters your attitudes and actions.

There are four important grammatical elements to consider in the command to "be filled with the Spirit" in Ephesians 5:18: (1) It is an imperative statement. This means that it is not a mere option but rather a *necessity* for effective believers to be Spirit-filled. (2) It is plural, meaning that it is for all believers who desire moment-by-moment submission to the Lordship of Christ. (3) It is stated in the passive voice, meaning that a source outside of ourselves does the filling and the controlling as we relinquish our wills. (4) It is a present-tense verbal action, meaning that it is an ongoing process. An alternative translation would be, "Be getting filled with the Spirit."

The Christian life is not a leap, a sprint, or a catapult from one special experience into another. The Spirit-filled life is a moment-by-moment walk with Christ. There is a conscious choice going on daily that determines who is in control of the Christian's life.

Scripture teaches that at the moment of spiritual birth we receive the Holy Spirit (Colossians 2:9-10). We do not receive Him in piecemeal installments. *All* the Godhead comes to reside in us, baptizing us in the Spirit. We don't just receive a partial residency of the Spirit in us. At conversion we receive an undivided God on a full-time basis. The "get more of Jesus" concept is erroneous. Everything we need is given at spiritual birth. The issue is, Will we allow the Spirit who lives in us to *control* us?

How can we know that we are controlled by the Spirit at any given moment? Apart from the inner assurance of our own sincerity of choice, is there an objective measuring stick? Yes, there is. Paul followed the Ephesians command—to be filled—with a simple but telling test of who is in control. Four participles comprise the test, giving an ongoing emphasis to the exam. The first in Ephesians 5:19 is *speaking*. How we use our tongue in respect to others is the first sign of control by the Spirit. Scripture describes twelve "one anothers," or dimensions of how Christians should relate to each other. Godly communication is a sign of Spirit-controlled living.

Ephesians 4:29 gives the standard of godly communication: "Do not let any unwholesome talk come out of your mouths, but only what is helpful for building others up according to their needs, that it may benefit those who listen."

Speech that is wholesome, positive, and uplifting eliminates slander, gossip, and character assassination. Pure speech is well-timed. It meets people's needs. God often imparts grace by bestowing a gift on an individual in a needy moment through a Spirit-controlled believer.

In our world of vile and unbridled language, a person with a pure, controlled tongue will stand out. And yet it is unusual to find people of pure speech, even among church leaders. In my opinion, the uncontrolled tongue has done more damage to the cause of Christ than homosexuality, pornography, or other current targets of Christian wrath. If there is any cause worth crusading for, it is the elimination of the uncontrolled tongue among followers of Christ.

The second participial command in Ephesians 5:19 is *singing*. This refers to an aesthetically sensitive worship of God. A Spirit-controlled believer is a worshiping believer with an attitude of praise and adoration toward God. The Spirit of God loosens our tongues for expression from the heart. A song in the heart is a sign of the Spirit's control.

The third participle in this test to show who is in control is seen in Ephesians 5:20: *giving thanks*. Here Paul says that we should be "always giving thanks." In 1 Thessalonians 5:18 he tells us to "give thanks in all circumstances." This kind of gratitude runs deeper than praise. It means thanking God in every situation—when I get a flat tire, when I'm late because of a traffic jam, when I'm fired, when my son gets three failures on his report card, when there is illness and death, when someone does me wrong. Paul is saying to give thanks in *all* things, not just the good things.

There is a difference, however, between giving thanks in every situation and giving thanks for an evil thing itself. When I learn that my accountant embezzled my life savings, I'm not thankful for embezzlement. But I am called to give thanks to God, for He is sovereign over the situation. Because I trust Him, I am convinced that He will turn the evil of the moment into something spiritually beneficial for me.

Difficult circumstances test our faith and produce character in our lives (James 1:2-4). Mature believers realize that "in all things God works for the good of those who love him, who have been called according to his purpose" (Romans 8:28). This verse doesn't say "*we see* all things working together for good," for, more often than not, we can't see beyond our trouble. But we can know with our spiritual perception that since God is God He will work it all out for our good—as long as we are godly and responsible throughout the course of our difficulty.

Thus far what we notice about the Spirit-filled person is his attitude. The Spirit-controlled person speaks to others in positive, edifying ways, sings with a melody in his heart to the Lord, and is thankful in all things because of a confidence that God is in control.

The fourth participle in the test is the most comprehensive: *submitting* (Ephesians 5:21). The Greek word is *hupotassō,* meaning to get into line under, or to take your proper position of submission. This concept of submission is further explained in the particular contexts of six of the most intimate, difficult, and revealing human relationships (Ephesians 5:22-6:9). Here is a telling look at life where we live, work, and play.

The six kinds of relationships are the relationships of (1) wife to husband, (2) husband to wife, (3) child to parent, (4) parent to child, (5) employee to employer, and (6) employer to employee. The personal test is to ask, "What am I like in the kinds of relationships that are most important to me? What am I like behind closed doors as I relate to my mate and train my children? How do I treat employees? Do I give my employer a full day's work? Am I rebellious or submissive, mature or irresponsible?"

The issue is our relationship to authority. The Spirit-controlled believer recognizes God's authority in his life and places himself in proper position. The husband has the key command to love his wife as Christ loved the Church. The husband who fulfills his role paves the way for his wife and children to fill their roles. In the same way, each person can influence the level of maturity and responsibility of others by his own mature approach to interpersonal relationships.

The key factor in maintaining a Spirit-controlled walk is (1) to have the will or desire to be controlled by the Spirit, (2) to choose God's revealed will even when it conflicts with our will, and (3) to keep on walking moment by moment according to our best understanding of His will. We can know we are filled with the Holy Spirit by taking a daily checkup on the Ephesians 5:18-6:9 passage. How is our attitude toward God and toward others? Do we evidence our love for God through a lifestyle of obedience?

✛ ✛ ✛

Knowing what it means to be filled or controlled by the Spirit is not enough. An understanding of how to continue this relationship is vital to our success. Such a committed, ongoing relationship with God is commonly referred to as *walking in the Spirit.*

Soon after a person comes to understand the filling of the Spirit, he realizes that the Spirit-filled life is not a sinless life. The most common Greek word for sin is *hamartia,* which means to miss the mark. For the Christian, the mark is "the glory of God" (Romans 3:23). Every person falls short of God's glory, for His glory is perfection. Perfection for the Christian in this lifetime is not an option on this fallen earth. *Progress* is a more appropriate descriptive word for the Christian life than is perfection. Until he goes to be with the Lord, the Christian will not become sinless. However, as he grows he will sin less. The concept that a person can walk in the Spirit yet still sin is found in 1 John 1:7-9:

> If we walk in the light, as [God] is in the light, we have fellowship with one another, and the blood of Jesus, his Son, purifies us from all sin.
>
> If we claim to be without sin, we deceive ourselves and the truth is not in us. If we confess our sins, he is faithful and just and will forgive us our sins and purify us from all unrighteousness.

Immediately after learning of the Spirit-filled life, many dedicated Christians jump right in with great zeal.

Unfortunately, after some time they become discouraged because of the guilt they experience in their moments of sin. Since they don't know how to handle the sin plus the guilt, they give up.

At one point in my youth, I sincerely dedicated myself to Christ, giving Him all I had. After a few days, however, I started to give up the Christian life, feeling discouraged and guilty. I gave up on Christ purely and simply because I did not understand walking in the Spirit.

The concepts of walking in the light (1 John 1:7), walking in truth (3 John 3-4), and remaining in Christ (John 15:5) are virtually the same as walking in the Spirit. When we "walk in the light," the blood of Christ "purifies us from all sin." The sin debt that separates the Christian from God has been paid in full by Christ's death on the Cross. We continue to sin subsequent to our salvation because we continue to live in fallen bodies. As we give these sins gradually over to the Lord, we are able to stay in fellowship with God. Only then can we be useful tools in His hands.

Here is a word picture that can help you understand walking in the light. Visualize yourself walking down a one-way path. This path represents the perfect life of Christ. As a Spirit-filled Christian, you endeavor to walk that very narrow trail. But because you're human, imperfect, and still dealing with the world, the flesh, and the devil, periodically you leave the path, stumbling off to one side or the other. On both sides of the trail are yellow lines warning you that you are about to leave the trail. If at that point you respond to the warning, correcting your direction, you can continue to make progress toward your destination.

The yellow warning lines are conviction points as you walk in the Spirit. If you respond to the conviction of the Holy Spirit when He tells you that you are about to leave the boundaries of the spiritual walk, then you can still remain in fellowship with God, continuing to walk in the light.

The action you should take at the conviction points is to turn down the temptation to go over the line into the territory of sin. But the action to take when you do go over the line and sin is to repent (turn back) and confess your sin.

The Greek word for *confess* in 1 John 1:9 is derived from two words meaning literally "to say the same thing." To say the same thing as who? The answer is the Spirit, who tells us that, indeed, we have sinned. You confess your sin, turn from it, and no longer desire to do it anymore. You then continue on down the path that God has prescribed for you.

Satan wants the Christian to wallow in the guilt of sin, not accepting God's forgiveness. That indicates how important confession really is.

It is vital to tie together the two concepts of being filled with the Spirit and walking in the Spirit. To be filled means to allow God's Spirit to be in control. In order to be Spirit-filled, we need our will to be controlled by God and to regularly confess our sins. To walk in the Spirit means to be continually under the Spirit's control. It means knowing how to respond to God when we sin and then knowing how to deal with our sin, thus moving on guilt-free.

When we understand walking in the Spirit as a matter of moment-by-moment control, much of the hocus-pocus is taken out of the Spirit-filled life. I think of walking in the Spirit on a practical percentage basis. When someone asks me how spiritual I believe someone is, I answer that it depends on what percentage of the time that person is filled with the Spirit versus the percentage he is controlled by the flesh. Some believers are controlled by the Spirit fifty percent of the time, others thirty percent, and some over ninety percent. The goal is to increase our percentage through spiritual maturity.

The practice of being Spirit-filled and walking in the Spirit are foundational to a successful Christian life. But there is one more major factor that should be considered. The general evidence that a person is Spirit-controlled over a long period of time is the fruit of the Spirit. The fruit of the Spirit is named in Galatians 5:22-23, following a discussion of walking in the Spirit: "The fruit of the Spirit is love, joy, peace, patience, kindness, goodness, faithfulness, gentleness and self-control. Against such things there is no law."

In a classic fruit-bearing metaphor (John 15:5-8), Jesus told His followers about the importance of being Spirit-filled:

> "I am the vine; you are the branches. If a man remains in me and I in him, he will bear much fruit; apart from me you can do nothing. If anyone does not remain in me, he is like a branch that is thrown away and withers; such branches are picked up, thrown into the fire and burned. If you remain in me and my words remain in you, ask whatever you wish, and it will be given you. This is to my Father's glory, that you bear much fruit, showing yourselves to be my disciples."

Walking in the Spirit, abiding in Christ, walking in the light—regardless of what we call it, spiritual continuity brings wonderful results. If a Christian abides, allowing God's Word to speak to him and talking to God in prayer, he will then become a dedicated disciple, giving God glory.

in his lifestyle (John 15:7-8). One of the resulting fruit for the believer is a deep, abiding satisfaction called *joy* (15:11).

In order to ensure that there is no confusion about what it means to be Spirit-filled, a quick review is in order. Every Christian is commanded to be filled with the Holy Spirit (Ephesians 5:18). There is no question that being Spirit-filled is God's will; we have the *command*. Second, we have a *promise* in God's Word that if we ask Him for something that is clearly His will, we will get it.

> This is the assurance we have in approaching God: that if we ask anything according to his will, he hears us. And if we know that he hears us—whatever we ask—we know that we have what we asked of him. (1 John 5:14-15)

We have the command *and* the promise. There is no way a sincere Christian can be turned down. It is ironclad. Once we are filled, we stay filled by walking in the Spirit. When we walk in the Spirit, we know how to respond to the conviction of the Holy Spirit. When we repent and confess our sins, God will forgive and forget, enabling us to move on guilt-free. As we continue to walk in the Spirit, we demonstrate that we are Spirit-filled by bearing spiritual fruit. Our close relationship with God is thus obvious in the most telling relationships of our lives, where we live, work, and play. The final authority, however, is the Word of God itself. During those times when we see no evidence of our Spirit-filling, we begin to feel spiritually inadequate, doubting our walk with God. At those moments we need to remember that God's Word is far more authoritative than any subjective experience or feeling.

There is no greater adventure than the Spirit-filled life. When we think and act correctly about that adventure, a life of joy and meaning is ours.

IV

RIGHT THINKING
ABOUT TEMPTATION

Sin is crouching at your door;
it desires to have you,
but you must master it.

Genesis 4:7

The British playwright Oscar Wilde summed up the attitude of millions when he said, "I can resist anything except temptation." Resisting temptation is no longer in vogue. Turning it loose is now number one on the libido hit parade. Restraint has literally gone the way of all flesh. Since the time of Eve's conversation with the serpent, mankind has been continually barraged with temptations. I read a few years ago that an average Californian driving more than ten freeway miles to work is subjected to over five hundred advertisements. The alarming fact is that the average person acts on seven percent of those billboards, bumper stickers, bus placards, and radio advertisements.

There are four basic responses to temptation. The

first is the most popular: *Give in.* If it feels good, do it. The second is the hardest: *Resist.* Fight it with every fiber of your being. The third is the procrastination method: *Wish it away.* Of course it never does go away. Fourth is the superficial response: *Underestimate it.* This approach usually leads to the ill-fated frog syndrome.

If a frog is placed in tepid water that is gradually heated to the boiling point over a two-hour period, he will eventually boil without ever desiring to jump out of the water. Because the gradual warming of the water is indistinguishable, the frog fails to realize his awful upcoming fate.

The gradual power of unresisted temptation can "cook our goose," spiritually speaking. The convicted embezzler could not have dreamed that the temptation of greed in the business place would overwhelm him, leading him to a prison cell. The loving father would have scoffed if initially told that his unchecked lust would eventually lead to the destruction of his family.

History testifies clearly about the effects of temptation. As a young man Napoleon wrote an essay on the dangers of temptation, yet in later years excess destroyed him. The Scriptures offer many examples of people who took their eyes off God as they submitted to temptation. David, a war hero, a popular king, and a man after God's own heart, allowed the power of temptation to scar his life (2 Samuel 11:2-5). Solomon knelt on the hillside of Gibeon and asked for wisdom, but later in life he foolishly married many foreign wives who worshiped other gods (1 Kings 3:4-15, 11:1-10). Peter, who uttered some of the Gospels' most profound statements, found himself on the wrong side of the fence from Jesus because he yielded to temptation (Matthew 26:69-75).

Temptation is powerful. It has struck down some of God's choicest servants. If David, Solomon, and Peter couldn't cope with it, how can the average person be expected to resist? In spite of the incredible power of temptation and our ineptness in resisting it, God still expects His children to win the victory. The first thing we must do is try to understand the nature of temptation. What is it, exactly?

The Greek word *peirasmos* is translated two different ways, depending on the context: (1) test or trial; or (2) temptation. In chapter one of James, the word is used in both different ways. The context of James 1:2-4 indicates external *trials* that come into a believer's life. There are certain ordeals that every person goes through that are not so much temptations to be resisted but difficulties to be endured. Personal trials—a death in the family, a business failure, a debilitating disease—are potential character-builders in your life.

James 1:13 refers to *temptation*, not to trials. A temptation, unlike a trial, is an allurement to participate in some sinful thought or deed. Temptation is the solicitation to do evil with the promise of benefit. In trials, the difficulty comes to us regardless of what we choose to do. Temptation, however, can be resisted. We are by no means powerless when we face it.

This week while driving to my office I encountered a temptation. There is a stoplight near my home that is programmed to change rapidly during the busy daylight hours and then slowly during the night. I came to the light very early in the morning when it was still on its slow program. I sat there for several minutes, looking in both directions. I was the only car for over a mile.

The temptation, of course, was to bolt through this seemingly endless red light—no harm, no foul. And that's what I did! I gave in to the temptation. If, while sitting at that stoplight, another car had slammed into me from the rear, that would have been a trial. But the urge to run a red light is a temptation. I have no control over a trial, but I do concerning temptation.

✦ ✦ ✦

It is one thing to know what temptation is. But how does it work? James 1:13-15 explains the dynamics of temptation. I call it *the evolution of sin*.

> When tempted, no one should say, "God is tempting me." For God cannot be tempted by evil, nor does he tempt anyone; but each one is tempted when, by his own evil desire, he is dragged away and enticed. Then, after desire has conceived, it gives birth to sin; and sin, when it is full-grown, gives birth to death.

The first word to underscore in our minds is "when." *When* we are tempted, not *if.* Temptation will always be present in the believer's life. A person who is no longer tempted has already been laid to rest. Temptation is part of the price of being human in a fallen world. There is no hiding place, no utopia where temptation is absent or benign. The presence of temptation is a fact of life for every Christian, so it behooves the believer to be prepared.

But when we consider the matter of temptation, we need to remember this scriptural warning: "When tempted, no one should say, 'God is tempting me.' For God cannot be tempted by evil, nor does he tempt anyone" (James 1:13). God is not responsible for the temptation that finds its way into my life. There are two facts that substantiate this principle. Although God cannot be tempted by evil, Jesus was tempted in every way that we are tempted (Hebrews 4:14-16). The words "cannot be tempted" in James

1:13, referring to God the Father, come from the Greek word *aperos*, meaning literally "unacquainted with," "without experience." God the Father is completely without experience when it comes to being tempted to do evil.

Because the Father does not possess a sin nature and does not experience sin, He cannot be considered a source of temptation. Since God can't be tempted to do evil, He will not tempt others to do evil. Therefore, temptation is never directed by God. The beleaguered Christian who is under the gun of fierce temptation must keep in mind that God isn't responsible for his plight, but that God *will* help him out of it.

While it is true that God is the architect of a plan that included the possibility of evil, He Himself is not the author of evil. There was certainly risk in the plan. Whenever an architect designs a building, he knows that, even though his plan is good and the building materials are solid, something may go wrong. How? Why? Because other people with wills of their own are involved. Thus he is not responsible; he is simply the author and facilitator of the plan. God is the perfect Architect and Creator of the universe; He has done this job without error. But man, who is the appointed workman in this universe, has a mind of his own. He is the one responsible for what goes wrong due to his own errors.

If God is not the author of temptation, then who is? Where does it come from? James explains the answer: "Each one is tempted when, by his own evil desire, he is dragged away and enticed" (1:14). Each person is thus responsible for how he responds to temptations. *We* are responsible, and we, together with Satan, are the source. John warns Christians to be alert to the world, the flesh, and the devil. A three-pronged attack on our spiritual lives comes from (1) the world system, programmed by Satan to work in his favor; (2) the fallen flesh, that spiritual pollution residing in man; and (3) Satan himself.

In James 1:13-15 the emphasis is on the flesh. James explains the origin and dynamics of temptation by employing a metaphor from fishing. Verse fourteen contains two Greek participles, translated "dragged away" and "enticed." The grammatical structure indicates that this dragging away and enticement is a continuous activity for the believer—the struggle of being lured by the subtle bait of evil. It is daily, it is distracting, and it is extremely difficult.

✛ ✛ ✛

There are four steps to the dynamics of temptation. The first, based on the fishing metaphor, is that *the bait is dropped into the water.* Just as the fisherman casts his baited line into the lake, so the world system, our own fleshly desires, and the powers of darkness cast temptation into our lives. The Christian, in this case, is the fish. He sees the bait as it dangles before him.

The second dynamic is that *we are attracted to the bait.* Why? Because of our "own evil desire." Every person takes into the new life in Christ the same flesh that characterized that person's unregenerate days. We all possess our own personal cesspool, the baser elements of our fallen nature in which we still sometimes indulge ourselves.

The flesh has an insatiable appetite. The more we feed it, the more it wants. The intensity of temptation is directly related to what we are feeding our flesh. If we are reading pornography, then Satan will drop the kind of bait that will intensify our desire for pornography. He will strategically exploit our weakness.

When a person fishes, he attempts to use the proper bait. It would be foolish to bait the hook with a light bulb or a nail because the fish would not be attracted to such bait. A knowledgeable fisherman has different baits and lures for different fish. His goal is to draw out the specific inclinations of the fish he is seeking.

The temptations that come to us are tailor-made by the enemy. Satan and his cohorts know us; it is their business. Thus they will drop the bait that best exploits our flesh. We should know ourselves well enough to stay clear of certain temptations that would place us in jeopardy. People have weaknesses toward overeating, gossiping, lying, wasting time, and thousands of other areas. The point is that Satan will use what we desire most in order to intensify our temptations.

The third dynamic is that *temptation turns into sin when we yield to it.* "Then, after desire has conceived, it gives birth to sin; and sin, when it is full-grown, gives birth to death" (James 1:15). The metaphor now changes from fishing to reproduction. Just as the man's seed comes together with the woman's egg, when we yield by taking the bait then *sin is conceived.*

I once counseled a young man who was fighting an intense battle with the temptation to attend X-rated films. The dynamics were as follows. Daily he rode home on the school bus, which stopped in front of an X-rated theater. Thus, step one, *the bait was dropped.*

He gradually found himself staring at the placards that were placed on the front of the theater to entice the public to enter. This was step two: *he took an interest* based on "his own evil desires."

As he became overwhelmed by the insatiable monster he had nurtured within, he finally yielded to the temptation by walking into the theater. Ben Franklin said, "It is easier to resist temptation at its inception than to satisfy its subsequent appetite." It would have been easier for the young man to resist the urge of his own lust than to fulfill the demands of a lust unchecked. Step three was now complete: lust had conceived, giving birth to sin. At this point there was a pleasure gained, but there was one more step to go—a step of diminishing return.

"Then, after desire has conceived, it gives birth to sin; and sin, when it is full-grown, gives birth to death" (James 1:15). Here is the final step in the spiritual declension. The offspring of lust is sin, and the child of sin is death. *Death epitomizes the overall negative results for the Christian.* It signals the end of a vibrant walk with Christ, an end to a sense of forgiveness, an end to a clear conscience and a spiritual mind. It leads to a life of guilt, shame, and depression. Hopefully this fourth step eventually pushes the troubled person to the counseling chamber.

It is critical for the Christian to understand and recognize the evolution of sin. The Christian is not an animal who operates according to an instinct over which there is neither responsibility nor control. God expects us to *see it coming.* Unexpected sin is not possible for the informed believer. Remember, step one: the bait is dropped; step two: our lust is aroused; step three: we yield to temptation; and step four: a complex of sin and spiritual death is the tragic result.

✦ ✦ ✦

The bottom line regarding temptation is our ability to handle it on a daily basis. Thankfully, Scripture states our primary guideline in one clear-cut verse penned by the Apostle Paul:

No temptation has seized you except what is common
to man. And God is faithful; he will not let you be tempted
beyond what you can bear. But when you are tempted, he
will also provide a way out so that you can stand up
under it. (1 Corinthians 10:13)

Three words jump off the page: "God is faithful."
This is a parallel to the passage in James 1. God's character
prohibits His participation in the origin or orchestration
of our temptation. God is faithful; He can be trusted; He
is on our side. Some think of God as a cosmic double-
agent who tailors temptations to us and then, at the last
minute, pulls us out of the fire with minor burns. God
cannot be tempted, He will not tempt the Christian, and
He will not lead us down the path to spiritual destruction.
He is to be fully trusted when we are tempted.

There is a triad of principles in this passage to be
branded upon our minds to help us handle temptation.
First, we must realize that *our temptations are common.*
Paul says they are "common to man." Temptation plays
games with the mind. In cases where a particular temptation seems unusually difficult, the afflicted person tends
to think his temptation is unique. Often our instant
response is to lament over the intensity and to allow
self-pity to weaken our resistance.

A good counselor will advise us in the midst of our
pity party that Jesus can feel with us when we are tempted,
that He understands. A relevant Scripture on this point
is Hebrews 4:14-16:

Since we have a great high priest who has gone through
the heavens, Jesus the Son of God, let us hold firmly
to the faith we profess. For we do not have a high priest
who is unable to sympathize with our weaknesses, but we

have one who has been tempted in every way, just as we are—yet was without sin. Let us then approach the throne of grace with confidence, so that we may receive mercy and find grace to help us in our time of need.

The thought that Jesus, too, experienced temptation is a helpful one. But at the same time we must remember that Jesus is God. Therefore, even though He was tempted, it was not possible for Him to sin. Nevertheless, Jesus Christ experienced real temptation, the highest degree that Satan could muster. Jesus can identify with us because He experienced greater temptation than any other man.

Consider the power of the temptation of good food facing Jesus after He had fasted in the wilderness forty days and forty nights. Think of the taunting of the obnoxious Lucifer, offering the motley barbaric kingdoms of the world to the King of kings. Temptation is somewhat easier to handle when there isn't much you can do to extract yourself from the situation. But for God Himself to be mocked and badgered by a mere created being—that was the height of temptation. The easiest thing to do would be to swat him down like a fly.

While hanging on the Cross, Jesus was taunted by lowly Roman soldiers who sarcastically cajoled Him to come down off the Cross if He was really king of the Jews. The truth is that only His love for the Father and the world kept Him on the Cross. The easy thing would have been to get off the Cross, slay the soldiers, and prove Himself the victor.

When I review the temptations of Christ in this light, I recognize that He can identify and empathize with me amid my temptations. Thus am I greatly encouraged. In contrast to His struggles with temptation, mine are minor.

Although each Christian has a distinct personality marked by unique strengths and weaknesses, our temptations are quite similar. Sex, money, food, material wealth — no matter what the object of temptation may be, people have more in common than not.

Whenever you think that your case is special and that no one understands, think first of Christ, knowing that He faced the same kind of temptation, and yet He did not sin. Also take heart that others are experiencing the same temptation and that many of them are beating it.

It is vital that in the heat of the battle there be no self-pity, which leads to self-indulgence. One of the Christian's best advantages is sharing struggles with spiritual comrades who will sympathize with and support him without overindulging him. Amid the daily pressures of temptation we can all receive help from the example of Christ, from the support of others, and from the truth that temptation is common to humankind.

The second member of this helpful triad in 1 Corinthians 10:13 is the fact that *we will never be tempted beyond our limits.* Paul said that God will not allow us to be tempted beyond what we are able to handle. There are many people who quote this verse but act as though it were not true. Whatever the temptation, God promises to give us the grace to endure the ordeal. One-legged cancer victim Terry Fox ran 3,339 miles across Canada before he collapsed short of his coast-to-coast goal in 1980. Plagued by pain and depression, Terry refused to give in to the long-distance temptation to give up. He typifies the human ability to continue past the normal limits of endurance.

A good friend of mine encountered a difficulty while working for a large corporation. His position came with a large salary, fat expense account, and many extras. However, an unexpected aspect called for in his job was the securing of prostitutes for foreign buyers when they visited this country. The temptation for him was to rationalize this role. He was pulled between the security of a good job and doing what was morally right, which was synonymous with unemployment.

When it seems that we can take no more, God promises to step in and give us the ability to cope. The demands in athletics call upon a person to extend himself beyond normal physical limits. The athlete is asked to run several laps, but after fifteen his feet burn, his legs ache, he is gasping for air, and he is about to quit. This is when the coach tells him he must run five more. Even though he feels like he is finished, he has more to give.

The marathon runner runs not only the 26.2 mile course but a whole gamut of emotions as well. The most important thing he must remember is "keep running." The runner knows that if he keeps putting one leg in front of the other, eventually the race will end. The Christian in the midst of agonizing temptation can be assured that God will ask him to run as far as possible, and no further. Sometimes we need to extend beyond our own estimate of our limitations. During those very difficult times, we must keep on resisting—in faith—until God rescues us from the temptation.

The third side of the triad on temptation is to realize that *God provides the great escape.* "When you are tempted, [God] will also provide a way out so that you can stand up under it" (1 Corinthians 10:13). There is no such thing as a temptation without an escape. Regardless of the intensity or the difficulty, any temptation can be resisted. Virtually every time I have given in to temptation, I must admit that I was not really looking for an escape. I would lament its difficulty, even rationalize its uniqueness, and then indulge myself. The one thing I didn't do was earnestly seek God's way out!

Potiphar's wife was constantly trying to seduce Joseph (Genesis 39:6-12). He resisted until the only choice he had was to sin or flee. There are various responses to temptations. The techniques we should employ are determined by the particular temptation. To certain temptations we are to show our heels. For example, we should "flee the evil desires of youth" (2 Timothy 2:22). It is not inherent in the nature of fallen man to last long in the face of sensual sins. Thus we need to make an immediate exit from sexual temptation.

Avoidance is another useful technique. Simply stay away from certain situations that will exploit your weakness. If you simply love ice cream, then don't go to the ice cream counter while you're on a diet. Don't "buy it for the kids" if you know you'll nibble. Cleanse your home of all ice cream.

Resistance is yet another method, and in most cases the *preferred* technique. Certain temptations can't be avoided. They are daily enticements where we regularly live, work, and play. But God is on our side. He will help us transform our temptations into victorious steps in our path of spiritual growth.

V

RIGHT THINKING
ABOUT THINKING

As a man
thinks within himself,
so he is.

Proverbs 23:7 (NASB)

There is nothing as easy as thinking, nothing as difficult as thinking well. The late Rufus Jones lamented concerning the intellect and the Church, "Whenever I go to church I feel like unscrewing my head and placing it under the pew in front of me, because in a religious meeting I never have any use for anything above my collar button."

Granted, Jones was going too far in his evaluation of the Church, but he did recognize a dangerous trend in religious life. The Canadian commentator Mordecai Richler wrote, "What scares me about the people of this generation is the extent to which ignorance is their armor. If know-nothingness goes on much longer, somebody will yet emerge from a commune having discovered the wheel."[1] These two opinions, one sacred, one secular, point out a growing weakness in both Church and society.

What scares me is the anti-intellectual, anti-critical-thinking philosophy that has spilled over into the Church. This philosophy tends to romanticize the faith, making the local church into an experience center. Further, it leads to faulty logic, particularly with respect to biblical interpretation. For example: God healed in the Bible; God healed me; therefore, God will heal everyone.

A balance is needed. We don't want fanatics of either the intellect or the emotions. Balanced disciples are vital to the spiritual health of the Church. A disciple is a cross-bearer, one who seeks Christ with a sense of deep commitment *and* spiritual stability.

Our experience-centered culture has greatly infected the Church. Many people have entered the local church to pursue happiness rather than Christ Himself. Their concept of "church" is that they are spiritual consumers and that the church's job is to meet their felt needs.

A church is not a place that exists primarily to make people happy. People with such a massive misconception of the Church often conclude, "I don't feel happy when I leave this church, so there must be something wrong with the Church in general." While the person's observation may hold some truth, the real problem is usually the erroneous assumption made by the happiness-obsessed critic. People who are constantly expecting a glow from glory or a zap from heaven have an insatiable appetite for special experience that can never be fully satisfied.

People who crave stimulating spiritual experiences often become trapped in the can-God-top-that syndrome. They need their weekly thrill to feel that God is still with them. The result of such experience-oriented living is either a feeling of frustration and guilt because God has seemingly lifted His blessing, or a tendency toward exaggeration of what is taking place in order to give credibility to the belief that He is still blessing.

In this atmosphere the pastor is viewed not as a teacher but as a devotionalist who tells tear-jerking stories that stir the emotions and make us feel either good or guilty. The *modus operandi* for growth thus becomes the escape-hatch mentality. Whenever there is a massive barrier that must be overcome such as an illness, a lack of biblical knowledge, a difficult mate, or a rebellious child, we are to "let go and let God." This entire experience-centered philosophy reminds me of a basketball team that spends its time practicing cutting down the nets and carrying each other around on their shoulders rather than practicing the fundamentals of the game.

These are simply a few symptoms of a much deeper inadequacy in the Church today. The real problem is in the mind. The most vital matter in the Church is the gray matter.

History demonstrates that the genesis of both wars and popular movements takes place in the mind—Hitler and *Mein Kampf,* Marx and *Das Kapital,* Mao and the little red book. Facism, socialism, and communism found their roots in the original thinking of men who published their philosophies. Ideas thus become ideologies.

While the mind of man is a marvelous thing, Scripture tells us that it is flawed. The mind outside of Christ is described aptly by the Apostle Paul:

> *A depraved mind:* Since [rebellious men] did not think
> it worthwhile to retain the knowledge of God, he gave
> them over to a depraved mind, to do what ought not to be
> done. (Romans 1:28)

> *A blinded mind:* The god of this age has blinded the minds of unbelievers, so that they cannot see the light of the gospel of the glory of Christ, who is the image of God. (2 Corinthians 4:4)

> *A futile mind:* So I tell you this, and insist on it in the Lord, that you must no longer live as the Gentiles do, in the futility of their thinking. (Ephesians 4:17)

There we have it. The post-Fall mind left to itself is *depraved*—unresponsive to morality; *blind*—unable to see God's workings and Satan's schemes; and *futile*—unable to develop philosophies that truly solve man's most basic problems. Although the innocent pre-Fall mind no longer exists, there is an alternative to the sinful post-Fall mind.

> Those who live according to the sinful nature have their minds set on what that nature desires; but those who live in accordance with the Spirit have their minds set on what the Spirit desires. The mind of sinful man is death, but the mind controlled by the Spirit is life and peace; the sinful mind is hostile to God. It does not submit to God's law, nor can it do so. (Romans 8:5-7)

The Greek word for *mind* in this passage is *phronēma*, meaning "a way of thinking" or "mind-set." In Romans 8:5-7 Paul was referring to the attitude or inclination of the mind. The unregenerate mind-set is hostile toward God, in total rebellion, virtually unable to submit to the authority of God. The self-made man is only a half-made man. He shakes his mutinous fist at God and says, "I'll do it *my* way!" Considering the alienation of man's mind from his Creator, it is not surprising that philosophers in general steer away from the biblical God. Regardless of how reasonable and benign human philosophy may appear to be, it dilutes and distorts the biblical message.

Some people teach that as soon as a person commits his life to Christ all things become new and the battle for the mind is over. Actually, the opposite is true; the battle intensifies. Instead of one, now there are two forces vying for control of the mind. For the enemy the stakes are now higher: For every Christian neutralized, there is one less voice for God. Not only is there a battle for mind control; there is also the vestige of pre-conversion baggage that is now transferred into the Christian walk. Feelings of inferiority, loneliness, and alienation regarding parents, children, and colleagues follow us into the new life in Christ. If we are emotionally unstable before Christ, we will probably be emotionally unstable post-conversion. The difference is that the new Christian possesses the power of the Holy Spirit, coupled with the truth of Scripture, to begin reprogramming the mind and controlling the emotions.

This combination of the new and the old creates the tendency in many believers toward double-mindedness. It is a kind of schizophrenia to believe one thing to be true but to practice another. The task of the disciplemaker is to teach new Christians to act on what they believe. But often we teach disobedience when our actions are not consistent with our beliefs. For example, we often challenge others to be witnesses for Christ when we do very little witnessing ourselves. We teach that we should love our neighbors as ourselves and love and do good to our enemies, yet most of us hardly know our neighbors and try to get back at our enemies.

The question must be asked: Are Christians in control of their minds? Do Christians think in a distinctive manner in this bewildering, corrupt world? Much of the battle for the Christian mind is subliminal, hidden below the surface. Since we know so little about the subconscious mind, we wonder if we can ever be certain that we are fully in control of our minds.

When we make decisions about moving, marriage, jobs, or investment of money and time, are we making mistakes? Do we really have God's leading? Should we consult Christian psychiatrists, gulp tranquilizers, or retreat to some wilderness until God speaks? The complications of the mind are staggering. In fact, excessive worry about any subject can lead to serious problems. To walk through life without certainty of divine guidance is nerve-racking. Many Christians are thus candidates for nervous breakdowns until they discover the secret of a dynamic mind.

A dynamic person is a product of a dynamic mind, which is the gift of the Holy Spirit. Thus every Christian can have a dynamic mind. Since the fallen mind is incapable of manufacturing such a dynamism, a transplant is required. Paul explains that transplant in 1 Corinthians 2:16: "We have the mind of Christ." Paul exhorts us to get this kind of new mind: "Your attitude should be the same as that of Christ Jesus" (Philippians 2:5).

The word "attitude" in Philippians 2:5 happens to be the same Greek root word that is translated "mind" in Romans 8:5-7. Both passages are referring to a certain mind-set or way of looking at life. There are two basic, very different mind-sets: The regenerate mind is set on things above, whereas the unregenerate mind is set against things above. A mind transplant is necessary for everyone. The incision is made by the will, and the transplant itself is performed by the Holy Spirit.

✝ ✝ ✝

The dynamic mind has three important dimensions. To understand what makes the mind *dynamic* we must have an appreciation of these three factors.

A)   *The dynamic mind is a spiritual mind.* —Paul explains that apart from revelation by the Spirit, our minds cannot know "what God has prepared for those who love him" (1 Corinthians 2:9). Why is this role of the Spirit so vital? "The Spirit searches all things, even the deep things of God" (2:10). Spiritual truth is found only in the mind of God. Only the Spirit of God searches and knows the thoughts of God. The Spirit of God is the only person possessing both the ability and the permission to search the mind of God. The necessity of our minds to be spiritually attuned is further amplified by Paul.

> For who among men knows the thoughts of a man except the man's spirit within him? In the same way no one knows the thoughts of God except the Spirit of God. We have not received the spirit of the world but the Spirit who is from God, that we may understand what God has freely given us. This is what we speak, not in words taught us by human wisdom but in words taught by the Spirit, expressing spiritual truths in spiritual words. (1 Corinthians 2:11-13)

Only the Spirit of God knows the thoughts of God; only the Christian has the Spirit of God; therefore, only Christians can know the thoughts of God. The purpose of the spiritual mind is "that we may understand what God has freely given us" (verse 12). God doesn't intend to play "I've Got a Secret" with the curious Christian —only with someone who refuses to believe. To the believer He gladly reveals information that is needed for walking effectively with Him.

The thoughts of God are not only *revealed* by the Spirit but are *taught* by the Spirit as well. The Spirit takes information from the mind of God, normally through the Scriptures, and puts feet on that information. The Spirit teaches us how to apply the thoughts of God in the market-place of life. The vehicle for this communication is *language*, as stated in 1 Corinthians 2:13: "expressing spiritual truths in spiritual words." The Holy Spirit utilizes the symbols of oral and written language to teach spiritual truth to His students.

Before a mind can be dynamic, it must be spiritual. Paul continues to explain:

> The man without the Spirit does not accept the things
> that come from the Spirit of God, for they are foolishness
> to him, and he cannot understand them, because they are
> spiritually discerned. The spiritual man makes judgments
> about all things, but he himself is not subject to any
> man's judgment. (1 Corinthians 2:14-15)

Spiritual truth slips through the mind of the unbeliever just as Jello slides between one's fingers on a hot day. There is no grid to hold it, no system to assimilate it, no way to work out in life what has been fed in. The goal of every believer is, as Paul puts it, to possess "the mind of Christ." To possess the capacity to think and act like Jesus in all aspects of life seems out of reach, but in reality it is as near as the Spirit Himself.

Capacity is one thing, results are yet another. The road to success is strewn with people possessing outstanding potential. Every believer, because of the resident Holy Spirit, has the potential for the mind of Christ. The percen-tage of Christians who actually obtain that mind or meaningfully move in that direction is small.

The dynamic mind is a renewed mind. —The next vital dimension is renewal. It is possible to have a renewed mind by allowing the resident Spirit to teach and apply the thoughts of God. Paul often refers to the renewed mind.

> Therefore, I urge you, brothers, in view of God's mercy, to offer your bodies as living sacrifices, holy and pleasing to God—which is your spiritual worship. Do not conform any longer to the pattern of this world, but be transformed by the renewing of your mind. Then you will be able to test and approve what God's will is—his good, pleasing and perfect will. (Romans 12:1-2)

Paul warns against being conformed or squeezed into the lifestyle of the world. The alternative to the big squeeze is the big change, which he calls transformation. *Metamorphousthe* is the Greek word used in verse 2 from which we derive our word "metamorphosis." Just as the caterpillar crawling in the dust is motivated to make its way up a tree to spin a cocoon, eventually emerging as a beautiful butterfly, so the Christian should be motivated to be transformed by the renewing of his mind. Spiritual growth of the mind is a supernatural ongoing process.

Paul elaborated further on the renewing process in his second letter to the Corinthians:

> We, who with unveiled faces all reflect the Lord's glory, are being transformed into his likeness with ever-increasing glory, which comes from the Lord, who is the Spirit. (2 Corinthians 3:18)

In this verse we see the same basic Greek word for change translated as "transformed." As the believer looks intently into the mirror of God's truth, it reflects back to him both the nature of God's glory and the condition of his own heart. Just as one makes adjustments after looking in the mirror, by God's Spirit the believer makes the proper attitude and behavioral adjustments. The mind acts as a computer: We place in the mind the thoughts of God and erase the false notions and assumptions from the unenlightened past.

The old things are put off, the new things are put on. True change requires not only ridding oneself of the old habit but also replacing the old habit with a new one. Otherwise, we sometimes revert to the former pattern. The renewed mind is a changed mind, changed by the teamwork of the Word of God and the Spirit of God. It gradually begins to take on the ability to deal with the world around it and to respond biblically.

The dynamic mind is a discerning mind. —

> Though we live in the world, we do not wage war as the world does. The weapons we fight with are not the weapons of the world. On the contrary, they have divine power to demolish strongholds. We demolish arguments and every pretension that sets itself up against the knowledge of God, and we take captive every thought to make it obedient to Christ. (2 Corinthians 10:3-5)

The real battle is in the mind. The Christian is immersed in an ideological conflict, even if he fails to recognize it. He receives daily input from both the world and, hopefully, the Word. The believer forms a defensive posture in order to ward off the Satanic salvos, plus an offensive strategy to take prisoners. Daily the believer is bombarded by the world around him, the flesh inside him, and the devil prowling about him. What he does with these factors determines the outcome of the struggle.

If there is no defense against the philosophy of the world, then the mind receives the world's garbage as readily as a funnel receives liquid. As a boy, I learned to make orange juice by halving the orange, placing one half on the squeezer, and pressing and twisting it until the juice, seeds, and pulp ran into the tray. Then I would take this mixed liquid and pour it through a mesh strainer into a glass. Only the juice could make it through the mesh. All other portions of the orange were strained out. The mind that is spiritual and that is being renewed will be forming a biblical straining system. Only those thoughts and desires consistent with Scripture will be received by the critical, discerning mind. The imagery used by Paul is that we take captive every thought to the obedience of Christ. The mind that is biblically quick will strain out what is false and harmful.

The shoddy thinking that is being done in our society is appalling. Many people employ logic and reason with utilitarian impulsiveness, thus rationalizing abortion, infanticide, premarital sex, petty theft, and other situationally expedient actions. Humanistic thinking always leads to man as the center. Whatever man desires or thinks he needs becomes paramount in all his decisions.

Even more distressing is the mushy thinking of Christians. The main reason Christian parents are frightened is that they don't have answers for their children. Oh, there are the stock Sunday school quarterly responses that usually don't even apply. But the parent who doesn't possess a dynamic mind shortchanges his children. The average cult member, having memorized three pages of stock answers, can twist the average Christian into a doctrinal pretzel inside of ten minutes. Discerning God's will, answering curious seekers, responding to crises, loving the unloving, and teaching the hungry have unfortunately been executed by a minute elite in the Body of Christ.

Christians need a mind transplant performed by the Spirit in order to gain a spiritual mind. To rebuild the mind we need renewal through reprogramming via the Word of God. Then this mind that is in the process of being changed by the Spirit of God must apply the new information to building a biblical strainer that will take every thought captive to obedience to Christ.

Every Christian should desire a dynamic mind, one that will form the foundation for a dynamic walk with God. A Spirit-taught mind, a renewed mind, a critical and discerning mind is a mind that responds appropriately and effectively to the stimuli of life. How can you achieve this type of mind? There is a certain vehicle that makes it possible to get there: "Do your best to present yourself to God as one approved, a workman who does not need to be ashamed and who correctly handles the word of truth" (2 Timothy 2:15).

As a Christian you are challenged to "do your best" — to take pains, to make every effort. This isn't just a suggestion; it is a command to study Scripture in a serious manner, to be a skilled craftsman in the use of God's Word. The goal is to apply the Word to life with a skill sometimes called wisdom.

Another Pauline statement relates at this point: "Have nothing to do with godless myths and old wives' tales; rather, train yourself to be godly" (1 Timothy 4:7). Training is discipline—the track on which the motivation and desire of the Christian runs. Many a believer gets charged up with a full head of steam like a powerful locomotive. But a locomotive without tracks churns itself into the ground. In a similar way, the highly motivated Christian without discipline ends up more frustrated than ever. In order to study, discipline is needed. The words discipline and disciple are related in that a disciple needs discipline in order to learn, grow, and become a laborer in the harvest field.

There are two ways to go as a Christian: the easy way and the right way. The easy way is living by our moods; the right way is living by our mind. The easy way is like a roller coaster ride where we strap ourselves in and relinquish control to the circumstances. There are incredible highs and depressing lows, but, regardless, we are not in control. The philosophy is essentially "Let go, let God, and be lazy." But the insubstantial nature of the Christian life ruled by mood rather than mind is illustrated in the life of Moses' sister Miriam and her friends.

> Miriam the prophetess, Aaron's sister, took a tambourine in her hand, and all the women followed her, with tambourines and dancing. Miriam sang to them:
> "Sing to the Lord,
>   for he is highly exalted.
> The horse and its rider
>   he has hurled into the sea." (Exodus 15:20-21)

The women, in celebration of the deliverance from Egypt, extolled the magnificence of God and played their tambourines. This moment of joy came easy, but three days later they were in spiritual despair, asking the question, "Is the Lord among us?"

Moses was less of a spiritual cheerleader than was his sister. It is not recorded how he celebrated, but it is a historical fact that he wrote books for the spiritual education of his people.

The tambourines were good for only a moment, but Moses' law was used for the next three thousand years. The emotion-ruled life is like a tambourine: It is not difficult to learn. Unlike the violin, the tambourine requires little training. You don't need to study at the conservatory or even read music to master it.

The scrolls of Moses are quite a different story. In order to master the law, one needs the discipline of learning the alphabet, grammar, logic, history, geography, and rules of interpretation.

But why are Christians called to mind over mood? Because the goal is to be skilled in the use of God's Word, which we need to understand in our minds. Only then will we see real change in our lives and in the lives of others. To "correctly handle" Scripture (2 Timothy 2:15) means to "cut it straight." It means to think biblically, to think as Christ thinks.

The premise of mind over mood is foundational. The mind provides a solid basis on which a person can live effectively for Christ. Emotional highs will come, but they are simply the extra benefits added to the staple of a working knowledge of God's Word and a mind that discerns the will of God amid a confusing world. Christians often reject the Word of God simply through neglect. The majority of personal conflicts and maladies afflicting the Body of Christ can be traced to an ignorance of the Bible.

If Christians would dedicate themselves to the diligent study of God's Word, the result would be spiritual dynamism. The key, then, is to make sure we are practicing the right kind of disciplines based on the right kind of thinking. It is a foolish actor who practices curtain calls but not his craft. The vehicle to a dynamic mind is discipline, long hours of study, constant learning.

When I sit down to a bowl of soup, I am interested in both nutrition and taste. If forced to choose between the two, I know the right choice to be nutrition. Oftentimes, however, I opt for taste. The Christian can choose between what causes growth or what makes for an emotional high. The nutritional value of soup can be likened to the spiritual sustenance of the Word of God and the principles that cause growth; the flavoring represents the emotions or experiential part of the Christian life. It is preferable to have both nutrition and flavor, but if only one is possible, the responsible choice is nutrition.

Only the vital principles of God's Word will see us through the difficult times. When it is time to make a decision, it is God's Word, not our emotions, that should dictate. For example, suppose I said, "I don't feel like attending church." Hebrews 10:25 gives me the solution: "Let us not give up meeting together, as some are in the habit of doing, but let us encourage one another—and all the more as you see the Day approaching."

And what does Scripture have to say about the statement, "Witnessing isn't for me"? Before He ascended into heaven, Jesus said to His followers, "You will receive power when the Holy Spirit comes on you; and you will be my witnesses in Jerusalem, and in all Judea and Samaria, and to the ends of the earth" (Acts 1:8).

Some people say, "I don't think I need to study the Bible." But the Word states, "Do your best to present yourself to God as one approved, a workman who does not need to be ashamed and who correctly handles the word of truth" (2 Timothy 2:15). "In your hearts set apart Christ as Lord. Always be prepared to give an answer to everyone who asks you to give the reason for the hope that you have" (1 Peter 3:15).

People who say "I'll never help anyone again because people are so ungrateful" should read the parable of the good Samaritan (Luke 10:25-37).

These are just a few examples of how God's Word speaks to our everyday attitudes and whims. When immersed in His Word, we are being exposed to His thinking.

Thus we can see through and correct the mistakes and the inconsistencies in our lives.

Dynamic minds are needed for a dynamic life in Christ. A dynamic mind is a spiritual mind; it is a renewed or transformed mind; it is a critical or discerning mind. The way to achieve this necessary mind transplant is through the discipline of study of God's Word and the application of the principles of God in life. There is no possible way to live for Christ effectively without a dynamic mind. There is nothing mightier in the hands of God than a Spirit-led person who possesses the mind of Christ.

NOTES: 1. John Stott, *Your Mind Matters* (Downers Grove, IL: InterVarsity Press, 1972), page 8.

VI
RIGHT THINKING
ABOUT FELLOWSHIP

How good and pleasant it is
when brothers live together in unity!
It is like precious oil
poured on the head,
running down on the beard.

Psalm 133:1-2

The Lone Ranger and Tonto, Huck Finn and Tom Sawyer,
Sherlock Holmes and Dr. Watson. Faithful friends—we all
need at least one, so we search and cluster in groups of
like mind to fill this need. Thousands of clubs, societies,
and associations have been established for people who
share common interests.

The Bible commands fellow believers to gather together. The Bible identifies a relationship called *koinōnia*
that refers to the close relationship or fellowship that
we have with other Christians. The Bible's definition of
fellowship is quite different from fellowship as it is commonly practiced. Usually when coffee and donuts are
served we say that we are having fellowship. But what we

often call fellowship should actually be called socializing.

Christian fellowship is to be distinctive. If we Christians are going to have fellowship as God intends, we need to know how it differs from society's brand. By asking a certain question you can tell if you are having true Christian *koinōnia*: Do you have open, honest communication with others about the essentials of life?

In order to distinguish fellowship from socializing, it is necessary to understand (1) the basis of Christian fellowship, (2) the primary elements of fellowship, and (3) the basic attitudes and actions of fellowship.

✢ ✢ ✢

(1) First John gives us *the basis of Christian fellowship*:

> That which was from the beginning, which we have heard, which we have seen with our eyes, which we have looked at and our hands have touched—this we proclaim concerning the Word of life. The life appeared; we have seen it and testify to it, and we proclaim to you the eternal life, which was with the Father and has appeared to us.
> (1 John 1:1-2)

This is what the Apostles experienced with their physical sensory equipment: what they could touch, what they could see, what they could hear—the resurrected Christ. Jesus was physically discernible not only during His life and His death but also during His resurrection.

Fellowship, according to John, is based on the reality of a shared experience:

> We proclaim to you what we have seen and heard, so that you also may have fellowship with us. And our

fellowship is with the Father and with his Son, Jesus
Christ. (1 John 1:3)

The Christian's relationship with God is the founda-
tion of his fellowship with other people.—The Apostles
had fellowship with the Father through the Son, thus
making possible their fellowship with other believers.
The basis of our fellowship with other Christians is not
what we have in common in the worldly sense. Quality
relationships with people on the horizontal can be achieved
only through quality fellowship with God on the vertical.
This is why devotions are so vital. The way we get to know
anyone, even God, is through communication.

We often tend to think that great relationships with
other people lead to a quality relationship with God. The
exact opposite is true: Only when we have a quality relationship with God can we have quality relationships with
believers. I once knew a man who was so very active in
the Christian community that he seemed to be everywhere
and to know everyone. He was a very social person, constantly on the go from one activity or function to another.
He desperately sought friends and the approval of those
he respected. But though he tried harder than anyone I
have ever seen, he had very poor relationships with people,
seldom even getting past the surface stages of friendship.

If Christians are not in the Word, not communicating
with God, then their fellowship is inevitably depressing and
superficial. A Christian who is discouraged spiritually, who
is frustrated with his own personal walk, will not be able to
be involved in the most rewarding aspects of fellowship. I
am not talking about a "down" day or even a discouraging
time of life; I am referring to a chronic lack of communication with the Father. Such a long-term vertical silence
sets up horizontal barriers between us and the fellow

believers who could encourage, comfort, and teach us.

We cannot depend on other Christians for our own vitality. We can't grow spiritually by osmosis. God alone has that kind of power.

John explains the hindrances to fellowship with God and with others in three verses: 1 John 1:6, 8, and 10. They all start with the words, "If we claim."

> *If we claim* to have fellowship with him yet walk in the darkness, we lie and do not live by the truth.
> *If we claim* to be without sin, we deceive ourselves and the truth is not in us.
> *If we claim* we have not sinned, we make him out to be a liar and his word has no place in our lives.

If we deny our sin, we deny the truth, thus giving evidence that we have erected a barrier between ourselves and God.

An honest, perceptive believer realizes that there is sin in his life. Paul wrote, "Christ Jesus came into the world to save sinners—of whom I am the worst" (1 Timothy 1:15). As Paul grew in the faith, he recognized ever more clearly the contrast between God's righteousness and his own meager efforts. Those submerged continents of lust, greed, and pride lay clearly before him. He gradually understood what he was really like. That is why he said, "I die every day" (1 Corinthians 15:31). He was not blind to the depth of his sin.

When we create a barrier based on denials of what we're actually like, we are sabotaging our own walk, clouding our judgment, and robbing ourselves of discernment. Then we eventually become defensive, projecting our guilt and frustration onto others.

The solution is in the alternate three verses: 1 John 1: 7 and 9, and 2:1.

> But if we walk in the light, as he is in the light, we have
> fellowship with one another, and the blood of Jesus, his
> Son, purifies us from all sin. (1:7)

As we submit to Jesus, He keeps on purifying us. As we
walk within the parameters prescribed by Scripture, we still
stumble and fall. Even though our intention is obedience,
our fallen humanity will betray our desire, and thus confession will be needed. As long as communication is ongoing with our Father and we are responding to the conviction of His Spirit, then we are walking in the light.
The primary relevant truth in this verse is that admitting
our sin and immediately dealing with it leads to a clear
channel of fellowship with God.

> If we confess our sins, he is faithful and just and will forgive
> us our sins and purify us from all unrighteousness. (1:9)

The emphasis here is the actual confession and cleansing. To simply agree with God that we have sinned is the
requirement. Honesty with God leads to fellowship with God.

> My dear children, I write this to you so that you will not sin.
> But if anybody does sin, we have one who speaks to the
> Father in our defense—Jesus Christ, the Righteous One. (2:1)

Not only should we walk with Christ and keep the
vertical channels of communication open, but when we
do need major assistance, Christ is available.

✦ ✦ ✦

(2) To separate fellowship from socializing we need to
know *the primary elements of fellowship.* I call these

elements *dynamics* because they do not take place in a stale atmosphere; they are fresh and flowing. Let's look in the book of Acts as we consider the early followers of Jesus.

> They devoted themselves to the apostles' teaching and to the fellowship, to the breaking of bread and to prayer. (Acts 2:42)

The Apostles' *teaching* was both the new information Jesus had given them and the Old Testament principles translated into the new economy of the Church. Then there were elements of *fellowship* (the personal interactions they had in common), *breaking of bread* (the meals they ate together and also the Lord's table), and *prayer*.

In Acts 2:42-46 we can clearly see the broad elements of fellowship. "All the believers were together" (2:44). This fact is fundamental, but often overlooked. Being together was a natural expression of a unique situation. Thousands of believing pilgrims were in Jerusalem from different lands for the festival of Pentecost, and they were totally captured by this new movement of Christianity. As a result, they lived together, shared meals together, took care of needs together, and thus set a fellowship precedent.

> Every day they continued to meet together in the temple courts. They broke bread in their homes and ate together with glad and sincere hearts. (2:46)

The "Love Feast" during those days was quite different from what we experience. The believers had an entire meal, followed by the Lord's Supper. It was such a special occasion that all the believers in the surrounding area came together for it. There are few things that break down barriers as quickly as the pleasant experience of sharing a meal.

"They devoted themselves . . . to prayer" (2:42). This

time of prayer was more than the pastoral prayer on Sunday morning. It was communal. Effective group prayer is accomplished by getting people together in small groups where they can pray over a long period of time with each other. People need time to get to know each other and to get over the superficiality and clichés. Gradually they start to be honest about their needs in their prayers.

Teaching, fellowship, breaking of bread, and prayer were four vital experiences in the early Church. The results were dynamic. "Everyone was filled with awe, and many wonders and miraculous signs were done by the apostles. . . . Every day they continued to meet together in the temple courts. They broke bread in their homes and ate together with glad and sincere hearts" (2:43, 46).

A positive, eager, enthusiastic atmosphere was developed because of many dynamic fellowship factors working together. That significant outreach resulted should come as no surprise. "Selling their possessions and goods, they gave to anyone as he had need" (2:45).

They not only met one another's needs but went into the surrounding community as well—"praising God and enjoying the favor of all the people. And the Lord added to their number daily those who were being saved" (2:47). They had the dynamics of fellowship going full tilt. It was a magnetic atmosphere. People couldn't resist it. They had to know what was going on in that place. People were showing their true love for one another—and as Jesus said, that is the most dynamic witness of all. "All men will know that you are my disciples if you love one another" (John 13:35).

✛ ✛ ✛

(3) When a believer has a right relationship with God and is involved in the proper elements of fellowship, the third

factor of *attitudes and actions* will be possible. Forty times in the New Testament we are told to love one another. There are ten specific actions that explain what loving one another means: devotion, honor, being of the same mind, acceptance, bearing burdens, friendliness, encouragement, giving preference to others, admonition, and prayer.

What must be permanently etched in our minds are the important foundation steps leading to vital ministry: study of the Word, prayer, fellowship, and witnessing. When these areas are strong, barriers fall and people begin to minister to one another.

+   +   +

The most neglected aspect of *koinōnia* is *accountability,* the mutual agreement between Christians to help each other obey God. Without some accountability, our spiritual lives remain undeveloped. Proverbs 27:17 speaks of one person's effect on another: "As iron sharpens iron, so one man sharpens another." It is good to have a friend to help knock off your rough edges, but such a process is possible only through a good relationship.

Suppose someone you hardly knew said, "Listen, after watching you I've noticed that you never seem to carry your Bible to church, you don't have a very good attitude, and you need to straighten up and walk with God!" You would probably tell that person to mind his own business. But if a close, trusted friend told you the same basic things in a loving and concerned manner, you would probably respond much better. In fact, you might even think seriously about his opinions and follow his advice.

The New Testament gives us over thirty words for ministry. One of my favorites is in 1 Thessalonians 5:14: "Warn those who are idle." The intention here is that a very strong warning is necessary. My own interpretation is, "Give people who are lazy a kick in the pants." This verse continues, "encourage the timid, help the weak, be patient with everyone."

> Let us consider how we may spur one another on toward love and good deeds. Let us not give up meeting together, as some are in the habit of doing, but let us encourage one another. (Hebrews 10:24-25)

Sometimes we need to be spurred on by being confronted in order to awaken us to our sin. Other times we need to be encouraged because we are defeated spiritually and emotionally. We need support and encouragement to keep going.

It is God's will that we have a group of people to fellowship with in a meaningful way. We need people with whom we can study, share, pray, and reach out.

VII
RIGHT THINKING ABOUT SELF-DISCIPLINE

*Like a city whose walls
are broken down
is a man who lacks
self-control.*

Proverbs 25:28

My greatest fear is that, in the end, my life will have been wasted. The very thought that the years God has given me might be futilely lost is repugnant to me. Most people feel a need to have worth, to distinguish themselves, to contribute to society, to leave their mark. Christians, however, hold a special need to make their lives count, because someday all will give an account to God.

In our society, purposeful living has become increasingly more difficult and elusive. The proper path of purposeful expression has been fogged over with Madison Avenue definitions of success. Advertisers have subtly deceived the world and confused Christians.

We are not alone in our fear. One of history's most

productive men, the Apostle Paul, was troubled with the question of purpose. There are several choice texts in which Paul wrestles with the issue of making life count, but none as memorable as 1 Corinthians 9:24-27:

> Do you not know that in a race all the runners run,
> but only one gets the prize? Run in such a way as to get
> the prize. Everyone who competes in the games goes into
> strict training. They do it to get a crown that will not
> last; but we do it to get a crown that will last forever.
> Therefore I do not run like a man running aimlessly; I
> do not fight like a man beating the air. No, I beat my
> body and make it my slave so that after I have preached
> to others, I myself will not be disqualified for the prize.

Paul illustrates purposeful living with a common denominator we can relate to: athletics. Every three years just outside the city limits of Corinth, Olympic-type games were held. The Isthmian games were kindred to the modern Olympics, with the primary events being various races. If you went to the site of these games today, you would find a once great stadium in semi-ruin. The masterful structure that could once seat more than fifty thousand is now the home of weeds, lizards, and occasional tourists. It is only a rough facsimile of its past. One remaining remnant of those days of glory is the line of starting blocks still embedded in the ground. You could stand in the middle of that once great arena and, with a little imagination, hear the cheers of the crowd and the grunting and groaning of the athletes.

First-century Corinth was as sports crazed as twentieth-century America. The nature of a foot race has remained the same through the eons. It's easy to draw conclusions from such a common occurrence. Metaphorically, life is a race in which there is a start, a finish, and a lot of challenge in between. In the Olympics very few compete and only one wins. In life, however, everyone competes and there are a great number of winners, but a great many losers as well. Therefore, since all of us are running the race, Paul's advice is to run it in a special way. "Run in such a way as to get the prize" (1 Corinthians 9:24).

Run to win, to grab hold of the prize. Fix your eyes on the finish line and plan to finish first. I long for that moment when Christ tells me, "Well done." Life is not a sprint; it's a long-distance race. And in this race every great runner has a strategy.

Last summer I ran in a seven-mile race. Frank Shorter, Bill Rogers, and other running luminaries were competing, along with five thousand others. I had trained for several months in preparation for this grueling experience.

When I arrived I didn't make my way to the front of the runners. There were markings that stretched for several hundred yards indicating anticipated running speed. I kept walking back until I found the sign marked "Nine-minute Mile." I had trained to run nine-minute miles, so I started with those who had trained the same way. I wasn't racing Frank Shorter, Bill Rogers, or anyone else for that matter. I was competing against the course and myself.

My definition of running to win was running to finish. My strategy was to finish and do the very best I could. I finished the seven miles in sixty-two minutes. When I crossed the finish line I was elated. It was a satisfying moment because my goal was achieved.

✦ ✦ ✦

Just as I possessed a strategy that led to the achievement of my goal, each Christian must possess a scriptural strategy that will ensure a life that is run to win, a life that will truly count. There are hundreds of tips that could be given on making our lives count, but Paul offers three that give us something solid upon which to build.

Paul begins his personal cameo on purposeful living by bringing up a very sensitive subject: *self-control.* "Everyone who competes in the games goes into strict training" (1 Corinthians 9:25). Self-control implies inner strength, the ability to curb life's appetites, control of the interior person. D.L. Moody said, "I have more trouble with D.L. Moody than with any person I know." The soft underbelly of Christian living isn't external trials and interruptions. Our vulnerability lies in our lack of self-control. How common are the inner disciplines of meditation, prayer, fasting, and study? Purposeful living requires this extra quality of self-control to cut the fat out of life and to give us a streamlined lifestyle.

The first-century athlete was required to train rigorously for ten months prior to the games. Training experts now tell us that if an Olympic athlete misses one week of training, he regresses eleven weeks. The inner stuff that causes one to stick with it must be there. The metaphor is enhanced by use of the word *competes* (9:25). This word means to agonize or struggle.

One of my former coaches prided himself in teaching his players the philosophy of pain. While we would stand on the end line of the basketball court preparing to run wind sprints, he would say, "First there is hurt; then pain; and then there is agony." He would blow the whistle and off we would go to test his philosophy. We would run until most of the team had reached agony. It was quite a sight to see grown men lying on the hardwood floor begging for mercy.

Just as most were at the breaking point emotionally and physically the coach would say, "Okay, fellas, five more sprints!" "What?!" protested several players. The protesters did run five more; those remaining quiet went to the showers. The purpose of this exercise was more than physical conditioning; it was emotional conditioning as well. Good athletic training takes athletes beyond their known limits so that they can cope with the rigors of actual competition.

Several weeks later this same team was in an exciting overtime game. It was down to the final seconds. The coach told us to run a play we had practiced several times. Every man knew his job. If all five of us controlled ourselves, the play would work and we would win. Four of us did our job, but one player lost control of his emotions. In an undisciplined frenzy he made a critical mistake and we lost the game.

As Christians, we dream of the glory of spiritual effectiveness. We admire Christians who distinguish themselves, just as sports fans look up to athletes. And yet we ourselves are often unwilling to pay the necessary price to be effective for Christ. The attitude among many Christians is, "I want to be mature in Christ and I want it right now!" But the Bible says we can't have full maturity right now. Being disciples of Christ requires long-term discipline. Paul taught this lesson about the importance of self-discipline in his first letter to Timothy: "Train yourself to be godly" (1 Timothy 4:7).

The writer of Hebrews gives further insight on the subject of long-term discipline:

> Anyone who lives on milk, being still an infant, is not acquainted with the teaching about righteousness. But solid food is for the mature, who by constant use have trained themselves to distinguish good from evil.
> (Hebrews 5:13-14)

We see in this passage that the cause for spiritual immaturity is *a lack of experience* (verse 13) and that the cure is *to get experience* (verse 14). The use of training is vital to our spiritual growth. Just as the athlete disciplines himself to train specifically for the events in which he will compete, the Christian must train in the kind of experiences that will take him toward his goal of godliness: study of the Word, prayer, meaningful fellowship, and witnessing.

Many people fail to translate desire into discipline. Desire itself is not a major problem for Christians. When we listen to an inspiring message, read a motivating book, or talk with an enthusiastic Christian, our desire goes sky-high. But desire does not equal discipline. Without discipline we are like a locomotive with no tracks, churning all our enthusiasm away without progress. As a result, we are more frustrated and discouraged than before. After a series of aborted attempts to make our life count, we exist in quiet despair, resigned to the defeatest belief that we can't do it.

While desire without discipline may destroy effectiveness and bring further despair, out of this despair new hope can be born. The vitally needed ingredient is self-control, an important fruit of the Spirit (Galatians 5:22-23). This seldom noticed fruit is commonly known as "and so on," with love, joy, peace, and patience getting all the reviews.

It is curious that self-control is overlooked and under-developed in the Body of Christ, for the character flaw most glaring among twentieth-century Christendom is the lack of self-control. The good news is that the believer need not be worried about conjuring up self-control because it is supernatural! No personal flagellation or sacrifice can produce supernatural self-control. The kind of discipline manufactured by the flesh is superficial, temporal, and oppressive.

To learn self-control we must make ourselves available to God. Before a pilot can engage the automatic pilot, he must first read the instructions on how to fly. The classroom instruction is followed by on-the-job training in the cockpit. In the same way, Christians must read the directions contained in the Word of God and then follow the directions by fulfilling the scriptural directives that come from God Himself.

Just as an apple is the organic product of an apple tree, spiritual fruit is the natural result of the Holy Spirit having His way in us. Fruit grows. Self-discipline doesn't mature immediately; it grows and fully develops over a period of time. There is no excuse for a Christian to complain, "I'm just not disciplined, so I guess the effective life must not be for me." Such an attitude indicates not only defeat but also ignorance. The disciplined life is within reach of every believer; God intends for every Christian to be effective.

God will help any believer who desires to make his life count. One of the most effective means is the encouragement of other Christians. There is no better vehicle for encouragement and accountability than the small group. It provides the personal touch. The small group is big enough to offer variety but small enough to keep a person from getting lost. Because relationships can be developed in depth, meaningful confrontation and exhortation can be accomplished.

The small group offers an atmosphere of acceptance where people can verbalize doubts, fears, joys, and concerns. Even when we wander back into old territory that hurts our walk, there is always someone there in the group to help pick us up and urge us on. This type of support group is the womb from which effective Christian living is born.

Most of us are like poor photographs: overexposed and underdeveloped. The quality of self-control can pave the way for making our lives count because it puts things back in balance and perspective. The reason most Christians fail is not for a lack of knowledge but rather for a lack of application. There is more to the purposeful life than self-control, but self-control makes moving toward the goal possible.

✢ ✢ ✢

The next suggestion by Paul on the subject of a disciplined life is *goal setting*. He states, "I do not run like a man running aimlessly; I do not fight like a man beating the air" (1 Corinthians 9:26). The trained runner competes with a clear goal in mind. The self-controlled person moves deliberately toward something specific. Although Paul's own objective is clear, many Christians unfortunately haven't the foggiest idea where *they* are going. Can Christians possess certainty in specific goal setting? Yes, we can!

Once again Paul treats us to one of Scripture's greatest purpose statements in a letter written from a prison cell:

> I consider everything a loss compared to the surpassing greatness of knowing Christ Jesus my Lord, for whose sake I have lost all things. I consider them rubbish, that I may gain Christ and be found in him, not having a righteousness of my own that comes from the law, but that which is through faith in Christ—the righteousness that comes from God and is by faith. I want to know Christ and the power of his resurrection and the fellowship of sharing in his sufferings, becoming like him in his death, and so, somehow, to attain to the resurrection from the dead.
> Not that I have already obtained all this, or have

already been made perfect, but I press on to take hold of
that for which Christ Jesus took hold of me. Brothers,
I do not consider myself yet to have taken hold of it.
But one thing I do: Forgetting what is behind and straining
toward what is ahead, I press on toward the goal to win
the prize for which God has called me heavenward in
Christ Jesus. (Philippians 3:8-14)

Knowing God—there is no greater purpose, no more
noble pursuit. Knowing God is a lifelong pursuit that
ends only in the presence of God. While this pursuit is
the bottom line of the Christian life, there is a way that
you can squeeze every last drop of potential out of this
pursuit: Establish specific goals.

Jesus specified the characteristics of a disciple in the
Upper Room: "If you remain in me and my words remain
in you, ask whatever you wish, and it will be given you.
This is to my Father's glory, that you bear much fruit,
showing yourselves to be my disciples" (John 15:7-8).

The disciple, according to Jesus, is thus marked by
four characteristics:

(1) *He abides in Christ.* The true disciple walks in the
Spirit. He walks "in the light," having consistent fellowship with Christ. The disciple communicates with God via
God's Word and an effective prayer life. God speaks to the
disciple regularly in the Word and the disciple talks back
in prayer.

(2) *He is obedient.* Jesus explained this obedient lifestyle to His disciples: "As the Father has loved me, so have
I loved you. Now remain in my love" (John 15:9). The disciple
thus demonstrates love for God through obedience.

(3) *He bears fruit.* Spiritual fruit is evidence that the
abiding and the obedience are valid. If the fruit of the Spirit
detailed in Galatians 5:22-23 are not present and growing

on a regular basis in the disciple, then he is a fraud.

(4) *He glorifies God.* This is the ultimate purpose of the Christian. The goal of God's redemptive plan is that God should get the credit.

There it is: a clear goal for every believer. First, abide via communication with God in the Word and prayer. Second, prove your love by obeying God's revealed will. Third, bear fruit, thus validating your discipleship. Fourth, the results are that God is glorified.

The Great Commission is to make disciples. Disciples are Christians who glorify God. Therefore, the goal of every believer should be to become a disciple. Serious Christians will set their sights on becoming established disciples who know God and glorify God.

The first step in goal setting is to *identify your objective.* Once the objective is selected, step two is to *set priorities.* In a sense, when you set priorities you show how much you really want to reach your objective. If someone says, "I want to be a person of the Word; the most important things in my life are family, devotion to God, and ministry opportunities," then that person's priorities should be rearranged to reflect those objectives. If the goal is to be a person of the Word, then study must find itself near the top of the list. It will force that person to seriously curtail other activities, such as television or socializing. Living with purpose means being ruthless at times in order to protect priorities. Getting sidetracked is the bane of the organized person. The good gives way for the best; the tyranny of the urgent must be abandoned for measured choice.

Specifying objectives and setting priorities are the easy part of living purposefully. The gaping crevasse in which many well-intentioned people are stuck is the gap between setting priorities and scheduling. A schedule is a device to help us get where we want to go. It is the test of the sincerity of our priorities. So I want to be a person of the Word? Where is it in my schedule? My experience has taught me that if I don't schedule it, it won't get done.

Sit down at the start of each week and write out a list of activities that must be done; then place them in your schedule according to priority. When trying to complete a project such as a book, I find it helpful to set a deadline. The next step is to plan the length of the book. Then I make a guesstimate of how many pages must be completed each week. This is followed by placing the necessary blocks of time into my weekly schedule.

Try the buddy system if scheduling is a new or difficult concept for you. One of the most productive activities can be sharing weekly schedules with someone else in order to gain helpful insight on being more effective. My wife was recently invited to join five women for breakfast. Their sole purpose for meeting monthly is to encourage and pray for each other's attempts to get organized and then stay on a satisfying schedule. If we desire to be effective, we must *plan* to be effective.

Because self-discipline, or self-control, is a fruit of the Spirit, it is within the reach of every believer. There is no valid excuse for soft, mushy Christianity. "I don't have any self-control" or "I don't have the time" are words that should never pass from a Christian's lips. The fruit of the Spirit are available to all who believe. Since we all have the same amount of time, the crucial difference is *motive*. When our motive is strong, then we will avail ourselves of the Spirit's self-control and will choose to use our time wisely.

✛   ✛   ✛

The third essential ingredient for purposeful living is *endurance.* Note the words of Paul: "I beat my body and make it my slave so that after I have preached to others, I myself will not be disqualified for the prize" (1 Corinthians 9:27). Paul brought his body under control of his spirit. The desires of the flesh didn't control him. He utilized his body to his advantage in order to reach his goals and fulfill his purpose. As he put it, "I . . . make it my slave." His body was prisoner to his life's goals.

Christians often allow the demands of the body to dictate priorities and time management. This has revealed itself in the preoccupation with maintaining lifestyles tailored by Madison Avenue experts who subtly create a materialistic appetite that only they can satisfy. Many Christians become so convinced that they, too, need certain worldly goods and services that pursuits such as evangelism, Bible study, prayer, and building relationships are squeezed out.

A Christian who wants to make his life count needs not only self-control and specific goals. He must also have the endurance to maintain a precise lifestyle for a lifetime. Self-control is an inner quality meant to harness the sensual appetites within. Endurance, on the other hand, is concerned with external forces that attempt to sabotage our progress. We can endure hardships because God enables us. Jesus Himself warned, "In this world you will have trouble. But take heart! I have overcome the world" (John 16:33).

In order to contribute a lifetime of purposeful living for Christ, you must have the toughness to take the bumps and bruises of battle. A.W. Tozer wrote, "I doubt if God can use a man greatly until he has been hurt deeply." God wants men and women sold out to the kingdom of God—with no strings attached.

"I myself will not be disqualified for the prize," said the Apostle Paul. Disqualified means "unable to stand up to the test." Just as metal is refined by intense heat, Paul realized that his life was being tested by great adversity. "If you falter in times of trouble, how small is your strength" (Proverbs 24:10). In other words, if you drop out when the bottom falls out of everything, then you didn't have much to begin with. Often the reason our ministry is either empty or nonexistent is that we are operating without the element of sacrifice. Not only are we aiming too low, but it is costing us too little.

The second book of Samuel tells a story of a nation in crisis. A plague had come upon the people of Israel. David wanted to make a sacrifice in order to stop the plague. When he tried to buy a piece of land from a wealthy man named Araunah on which to build the altar, Araunah offered the land, the oxen, and whatever else he needed as a gift. But David's answer to him was simple and clear: "No, I insist on paying you for it. I will not sacrifice to the Lord my God burnt offerings that cost me nothing" (2 Samuel 24:24).

The service that costs is the service that counts. Effective service for Christ doesn't come at bargain basement prices. The life that leaves its mark is one characterized by dedication and sacrifice.

Paul desired to win the prize, the imperishable wreath (1 Corinthians 9:24-25). He did not want to be disqualified (9:27). Rather, he longed for a life that would count in the long run. At the end of his life, he apparently possessed this kind of assurance.

I am already being poured out like a drink offering, and the time has come for my departure. I have fought the good fight, I have finished the race, I have kept the faith. Now there is in store for me the crown of righteousness, which the Lord, the righteous Judge, will award to me on that day—and not only to me, but also to all who have longed for his appearing. (2 Timothy 4:6-8)

What peace of mind—to know at the end of one's life that God's will was done. That is the greatest sense of accomplishment known to man.

This same assurance can be yours. It is within reach of every Christian. But it will take self-control, which is a fruit of the Spirit; it will take specific goals based upon Scripture; and it will take endurance to reach your destination.

VIII
RIGHT THINKING ABOUT THE WORD

*Your word is
a lamp to my feet and a
light for my path.*

Psalm 119:105

The greatest issue facing the Church today is not the integration of politics and faith or the social application of the gospel. The axis on which the Church must turn is the Christian's relationship to the Bible. Most Christians do claim to believe the Bible. After all, the average American home has four Bibles. Many people believe that the Bible is the Word of God. What we believe about the Bible is a start, but what we do with it is far more important.

While I was growing up, there was a large family Bible on the living room coffee table of our home. It was a cherished family heirloom, filled with important photos, certificates, birth and death information. Although many things were done with that family Bible, it was not read!

Fewer than fifty percent of evangelicals read the Bible daily. Only ten percent are able to identify the location of Jesus' discussion with Nicodemus; fewer than forty-two percent can name five of the Ten Commandments. It is frightening that many of the forty million evangelicals in our nation are biblically illiterate. Thus, even though interest in religion is on the increase, ethically and morally it is making little difference.

We often treat the Bible as a religious scrapbook. We leaf through the pages and fondly remember bits and pieces of favorite verses. It is our spiritual Aladdin's lamp. We rub it just right and say the magic words and out pops the answer of the hour. The other extreme is to treat it like a textbook. We master the minutiae, debating biblical trivia and priding ourselves on our voluminous knowledge.

One word that describes the desired balance between neglect of the Word and abuse of the Word is *hunger*. "Like newborn babies, crave pure spiritual milk, so that by it you may grow up in your salvation, now that you have tasted that the Lord is good" (1 Peter 2:2). One of the greatest issues facing the Church is the lack of hunger for God's Word. Consider a baby's desire for milk. A baby will not take no for an answer. His screaming protest is intense and unrelenting. Just as that baby's hunger for milk is innate, intense, and unassailable, so should the Christian's hunger be.

Just as naturally as a child takes to the breast, a Christian takes to the Word. Both our breast-fed sons went through a phase during which, like Pavlov's dogs who were conditioned to eat at the sound of a bell, they became fussy and hungry at the sound of my wife's voice. If she merely held them, they thought it was dinner time. It was when they loudly demanded middle-of-the-night meals that she wished God had shared feeding privileges with males.

Sometimes Jane and I talk about how glad we are that those days are over. But for the Christian the days of feeding on spiritual milk should never end. Peter refers to a lifelong hunger for God's Word that is innate, intense, and unassailable. Of course, he wouldn't *command* it if it were easy to maintain. Like any other quality, it must be nurtured.

Many Christians fondly reflect back on those days in Christ when they eagerly arrived early, sitting in the front of the church, poised on the edge of the pew, hanging on every word the pastor said. But now they find themselves in the back row just hanging on to consciousness. The deceptive concept that interest in the Bible inevitably wanes as we grow older in Christ has been swallowed whole by many Christians. When the older Christian comments that the enthusiasm of the naive new believer will eventually fade, he is injecting poison into the health of the church. The opposite is actually true: The more we feed on the Word, the greater will be our hunger.

What should be done when spiritual hunger seems to have disappeared? Well, what happens when a child loses his appetite? It is assumed that he is sick. Something is wrong, and so medical attention is sought. If we have lost our hunger for spiritual food, then we are spiritually sick. In fact, regarding the eternal effect, lack of spiritual hunger is far more serious than lack of physical hunger.

The reason for gross neglect of spiritual nourishment is twofold. First, lack of spiritual hunger is an epidemic of such vast proportions that it is generally accepted as a normal spiritual state. Second, it brings delayed consequences—effects that are not immediately manifested or easily detected.

Various substitutes are being used to fill the void. Children are warned not to use junk food as a staple for nutrition. When a child fills up on cupcakes and cookies, chasing them down with a root beer, he loses his appetite for salad, vegetables, and important body-building foods. Christians, too, are fed a junk food diet by both the world and the Church. The world offers a steady diet of inane, immoral television shows, books, magazines, and films that present presumably valid alternative lifestyles and moral options to the young. The Church offers pop psychology and sermons catering to the niceties of the flesh rather than the principles of God's Word.

A spiritual loss of appetite is a serious thing. We need spiritual nourishment in order to *grow up* in our salvation (1 Peter 2:2). In other words, if we stop eating, we stop growing! If the appetite is lost, the first order of business is to rid oneself of whatever has destroyed the appetite. In the human body the culprit is often a virus. A spiritual infection is mentioned in 1 Peter 2:1: "Rid yourselves of all malice and all deceit, hypocrisy, envy, and slander of every kind." Get rid of it! Instead of malice, try ministry; instead of deceit, try speaking the truth in love; instead of hypocrisy, try consistency; instead of envy, try rejoicing in other people's success; instead of gossip, try praying for others. These are the alternatives the Word offers.

A positive sign following a bout with a viral infection is the return of one's appetite. The person who begins to rid himself of spiritual poisons will begin to hunger for God's Word and understand it in a new light.

Once the poison has been removed, how can a hunger be developed? Proverbs 22:6 helps at this point: "Train a child in the way he should go, and when he is old he will not turn from it." The Hebrew word translated "train" has an interesting history. When a Hebrew child was born, the midwife would immediately dip her fingers in a solution of crushed dates and rub them on the roof of the child's mouth. This would give the baby a desire to nurse, and thus nourishment was assured. The word itself could be translated "create a thirst." The godly parent is called to create a thirst in his child for spiritual life.

> These commandments that I give you today are to be upon your hearts. Impress them on your children. Talk about them when you sit at home and when you walk along the road, when you lie down and when you get up. Tie them as symbols on your hands and bind them on your foreheads. Write them on the doorframes of your houses and on your gates. (Deuteronomy 6:6-9)

Here we see that the most effective method of creating this spiritual thirst is modeling. The example of the parent is life's most effective teaching tool. The Christian parent is to model the reality of Christ and the relevance of His Word. If a child is taught that knowing Christ is a positive, liberating experience and that His Word is the most exciting book known to man, then he will indeed thirst for it.

The first week we were married my wife cooked meat loaf. What she didn't know was that I hated meat loaf. I couldn't stand the sight or smell of that unsavory substance. When she told me we were having meat loaf I thought she was kidding. I raced to the oven exclaiming that she surely couldn't be so cruel as to do that to good hamburger. I couldn't eat it; I didn't even attempt it. My wife didn't mind; she wasn't crazy about meat loaf, either.

Four years later I sat down at the dinner table and my eyes beheld a delightful meal. The meat was some type of beef laced with onions, grated carrots, and cheese, topped with a red sweet-and-sour sauce. In accompaniment was my favorite cheesy potato casserole. After the meal I commented how wonderful everything had been. I asked what she called the meat dish, which was so good. "Meat loaf," she grinned. I was shocked, but I had to admit she disguised it beautifully. I had downed three helpings.

If the Word of God is taught properly, pleasant to the eye and ear, Christendom would be surprised how people would "eat it up." This is Peter's comment in 1 Peter 2:3: ". . . now that you have tasted that the Lord is good." If the Word was taught in our homes and churches in a delightful way that could be consumed at every age level, there would be far more hungry hearts. Children, for example, learn better from visual and tactile experiences. They identify well with the fall of Jericho if they can build a toy city and march around it, watching it collapse. They can remember something concrete like that.

We have a responsibility to create a thirst for God's Word first by modeling the reality of Christ; second, by coaxing and encouraging people to read and study Scripture; third, by decorating the Word for delectability.

In the end, we are talking about motivation. The Veterans' Hospital in Long Beach, California, attempted to improve emergency procedures by practicing fire drills. The new record for evacuating the building was a snappy six minutes. What startled some observers, however, was that when quitting time came for employees to go home, it took only three minutes for them to get out of the building. *Motivation* is the key. Create a thirst or a hunger by getting rid of what is wrong and then putting in what is right.

✦ ✦ ✦

A hunger for God's Word is important because our goal is that all Christians may be both nourished and equipped. In the physical realm, a good diet along with moderate exercise creates a healthy appetite. Under such positive circumstances, a self-perpetuating cycle is established. The body burns calories, desires and eats food, feels good, burns more calories, then demands more food, ad infinitum.

In the spiritual realm, however, the cycle of appetite, exercise, increased appetite, more exercise, etc. is more easily broken. Several years ago I was responsible for the training of fifteen missionaries. Part of the training was a daily Bible study. After a week of reviewing the basic doctrines of Scripture, the trainees began to complain, asking me to teach the deeper truths. I simply told them to meet me the next morning at the same time.

The next morning at the appointed time we filed into three cars and headed for the skid row section of our city. When quizzed as to the purpose of our field trip, I told them we were going to witness to the winos on skid row to find out how much we really knew. The following day these former know-it-alls showed up for Bible study with notebooks filled with questions that needed answers. One day debating with men who had pondered many of life's most difficult questions created an intense hunger to study the Bible. They finally felt a strong need. Gone were the pat answers, the intellectual snobbery, and the finicky appetites.

The need for the Word doesn't come from the desire to be nourished but rather from the need to be sustained. When we Christians are exercising our faith, when we are on the front lines for Christ, we won't just have a casual interest to study the Bible; we will be desperate for it.

Another reason we need the Word is to be equipped

for ministry. "All Scripture is God-breathed and is useful for teaching, rebuking, correcting and training in righteousness, so that the man of God may be thoroughly equipped for every good work" (2 Timothy 3:16-17). Scripture helps us stay in mint condition so that we can have full fellowship with Christ and with other Christians. We all need to be thoroughly equipped in order to live the Christian life effectively and to labor in the harvest field.

These verses indicate a four-fold ministry for Christians that is undergirded by Scripture: teaching, reproof, correction, and training. *Teaching* is a course of action that looks outward toward others. The life of Christ is our model of showing others how to put right thinking into right action.

But because we are human and sinful, we wander off the perfect path of prescribed holiness, thus necessitating the second ministry of the Word. *Reproof* is the Spirit of God telling me, via His Word, that I have erred and that corrective action must be taken immediately.

Correction, the third phase of the Word's ministry, is a course of action. God's Word corrects my path by pointing me in the proper direction.

The fourth and final phase is *training*. Now that my wandering has been corrected, I need to stay on the path. The Word acts as a trainer. I can learn a new habit pattern or attitude because the Word gives me the information, the motivation, and the how-to so that it can be accomplished.

God's Word serves as an equipper and transformer of both mind and action. It prepares the Christian for obedience, for ministry, and for holding life together in the midst of a turbulent world.

How can the Church create a hunger for God's Word so that the believer can be both nourished and equipped?

The Scripture itself answers the question. The Bible states five basic ways for people to relate to the Word of God.

✝ ✝ ✝

(1) The first level is *listening to the Word.* Romans 10:17 refers to the value of listening: "Faith comes from hearing the message, and the message is heard through the word of Christ." Listening to the Word as it is taught is the least demanding yet least understood way to relate to Scripture. Sunday after Sunday, people listen to sermons. Some people have listened to sermons most of their lives. Amid the present glut of sermonic offerings via the media, the Christian is not hard-pressed to find a sermon. The help we gather from sermons depends on how well we listen and how well we evaluate what we have heard.

Unfortunately, Christians often listen to sermons through a worldly filter. Generally we rate a sermon according to whether or not we enjoyed it—its entertainment value. "Did it have good stories that made me laugh or cry? Was the speaker's voice pleasant to the ear? How were his mannerisms? What was his personality like? Did I care for his delivery?" Then, of course, there will be comparisons made: "Well, he certainly isn't as good as Dr. Decipher or Pastor Panache."

We have become a nation of sermon tasters. Many of us approach a sermon as though we were daring the speaker to bless us. Often we approach the message either coldly, critically, or casually. This is one key area in which the Church has become rather worldly: when messages from God's Word are treated with disdain. Frankly, this attitude is an abomination to the Lord.

The first way to evaluate any message is clear-cut: Does the speaker use the Bible? The foundation of the sermon or Sunday school lesson must be Scripture. If the Bible is not being used, the lesson usually has little value.

Next, is the message accurate? Does it faithfully reflect the text being used? Even though accuracy can be a sticky issue, the sincere attempt to present the true message of the text should be evident.

Another indication of a solid message is clarity. Does the message cut through the fog of religious language and side issues in a way that is understandable? The message must make good sense in order to gain credibility with the discerning listener.

One more important indicator is practicality. Does the message translate into the marketplace, work place, and home place? An impractical truth is not necessarily useless. But if it is indeed truth, feet can probably be put on it, enabling it to walk into our lives. Not all truth is immediately usable. But we can look toward future use. The speaker should always attempt to relate biblical truth to practical situations such as marriage, child rearing, business ethics, relationships, and society's important moral issues.

When someone stands before Christians with a Bible in hand and a message on his heart, a holy moment is established. Whenever a person who is Spirit-filled teaches the Bible to Spirit-filled listeners, God has promised to speak. There is no such thing as a useless message if God's Word and God's Spirit are present and if people truly desire to learn. When the Word is opened and taught, we should be prepared to hear God speak.

American philosopher Mortimer Adler has done us a great service by speaking about passive versus active listeners.[1] The passive listener has not yet learned to listen and gets very little from whatever is presented. The active listener, however, takes notes and is totally involved in what is being said. Every Christian should bring a Bible to church. During the message, the Bible should be open, and beside the Bible should be a note pad. Taking notes raises retention from the passive listener's level of ten percent to the active listener's level of fifty percent. Even if the note taker throws the notes in the trash basket on the way out, he has learned far more than he would have otherwise.

Active listening is good listening. Asking questions and reviewing tapes and notes of messages will make us even better listeners. Since Christians spend so much time listening to sermons, it is clearly prudent for us as good stewards of our time to listen well.

+ + +

(2) The second level of relating to Scripture is *reading the Word*. Revelation 1:3 indicates the benefits of reading: "Blessed is the one who reads the words of this prophecy, and blessed are those who hear it and take to heart what is written in it, because the time is near."

Again we can take Adler's advice on the value of learning to read a book actively rather than passively. Active reading means underlining, making notes in the margins, and then rereading the book and writing out meaningful principles that can be applied.

Reading the Bible should be a daily activity for our own personal edification. Many reading programs are available to the person who desires to read the entire Bible in one year. My recommendation is to read at your own pace and enjoy what God has to say. Every Christian needs a daily feeding on the Word. This is part of the Christian's discipline and joy. Years ago I came across some good advice: Read the Bible as a means to fellowship rather than a means to scholarship.

✛ ✛ ✛

(3) The next level of commitment to Scripture is *studying the Word.* "Do your best to present yourself to God as one approved, a workman who does not need to be ashamed and who correctly handles the word of truth" (2 Timothy 2:15). "Do your best" means to be dedicated. Put forth a real effort to study Scripture. Whereas reading the Word is preferably a daily activity, study should also be a fairly regular activity, two or three times per week.

The difference between reading and studying is the retention level. Active reading involves underlining, notes in the margin, and sometimes rereading. Study calls for repetition, concentration, reflection, and mental application. Study begins where reading leaves off. Study is an investigation of the essence of truth that will eventually be used in teaching others. It has a double goal: to edify the student and then to edify and instruct others later on.

The local church should be a study center. Sunday school classes should be demanding, covering the meatier aspects of spiritual truth. There is no shortage of Christian books, tapes, and helpful literature.

Churches need strong libraries that have the best literature available. This library should be promoted weekly through the bulletin, newsletter, or bulletin board. Since women already buy and read eighty percent of the Christian books being sold, men should be targeted to start reading. Zero in on men who have an interest to study but who have failed to schedule study time. Small study groups can be organized where mutual encouragement and accountability are present.

Paul admonished Timothy, "Do your best to present yourself to God as one approved, a workman who does not need to be ashamed. . . ." Many Christians are rightfully ashamed of their lack of knowledge. The general intellectual ineptness of the Church is a shame to its members and a blot on the name of Christ. Therefore, we should make every effort to stem the tide, and encourage others to follow suit.

✛ ✛ ✛

(4) The next level of relating to Scripture is *memorizing the Word.* "How can a young man keep his way pure? By living according to your word. . . . I have hidden your word in my heart that I might not sin against you" (Psalm 119:9,11). Saturating the mind with Scripture helps keep us from sin. If that's not enough motivation, then 2 Corinthians 10:3-5 should help:

> Though we live in the world, we do not wage war as the world does. The weapons we fight with are not the weapons of the world. On the contrary, they have divine power to demolish strongholds. We demolish arguments and every pretension that sets itself up against the knowledge of God, and we take captive every thought to make it obedient to Christ.

Aligning every thought with the thinking of Christ is crucial to effective Christian living. There are various times when we are dealing with temptation or confrontation with enemies of the gospel when a Bible or sermon notes are not readily available. Having Scripture in the mind, at our mental fingertips, will help keep us from sin and serve us well in discussing the issues of the gospel. The

Topical Memory System published by NavPress is an effective tool for committing Scripture to memory in an orderly way.

✦ ✦ ✦

(5) In some ways the most advanced aspect of relating to Scripture is *meditating on the Word.*

> Do not let this Book of the Law depart from your mouth; meditate on it day and night, so that you may be careful to do everything written in it. Then you will be prosperous and successful. (Joshua 1:8)

Eastern mysticism has given meditation a bad name. Eastern religions utilize meditation to empty the mind, whereas Christian meditation calls us to fill the mind. The Hebrew word for "meditate" here is derived from a word for a cow chewing her cud. As a cow chews and rechews the same material, so the meditator of the Word spends a great deal of time on the same passage or topic of Scripture until it has sufficiently assimilated into his mind.

In order to meditate, we first must be willing to memorize. The Scripture we are working on must be extremely familiar before we can truly concentrate on its meaning. Once we have memorized a passage, then we can visualize it. For example, we can picture the feeding of the five thousand: the disciples doubting that enough food could be found, the little boy giving all he had, Andrew doubting, Philip calculating, Jesus smiling, then the multiplication of five loaves and two fish, the filled bellies of thousands, and the twelve disciples struggling to carry the baskets of leftovers.

Next, we personalize. How does this relate to me?

How can I use these principles in my daily life? Possibly the application would be that the people God has given me to work with are my loaves and fishes. Like the little boy, I give God my best —that is all He ever asks. He then takes my best and multiplies it twenty-fold, possibly more. Meditation can serve to enlighten us in ways that hurried study or reading would never yield.

A warning: Some Christians advocate out-of-the-body experiences in meditation. There are danger areas that need to be avoided. First, any experience that directly contradicts Scripture is a false and precarious experience. Second, any occultic manifestations such as strangely moving objects, visions or voices of spirit beings, or out-of-the-body experiences such as astral projection, are unequivocally to be avoided.

✦ ✦ ✦

World starvation is tragic. Often we hear reports that thousands starve to death daily. Television specials on the troubles and tragedies of the world break our hearts. The ghettos of our own country, where poverty, illiteracy, child abuse, and neglect are a legacy, are a national sore that won't heal.

But as sad as this conglomerate of pathos and injustice is, there is an even greater tragedy. We should be weeping for ourselves. The Christian community is a starving people, an illiterate people. Our ranks are laced with a legacy of frustration and discontent. And there has been a general acceptance of our spiritual poverty among ourselves that only the eye of the Spirit can see.

The only cure is a hunger for God's Word. God's people need to take the study and application of His truth seriously. Those of you reading this can begin, in the tradition of Ezra, to devote yourselves to the study, practice, and teaching of the Word (Ezra 7:10). Get hungry, Christian. Take, eat, and learn of Him.

NOTES: 1. I recommend *How to Read a Book* by Mortimer Adler, published by Simon & Schuster, Inc.

IX

RIGHT THINKING
ABOUT PRAYER

The Lord is near
to all who call on him,
to all who call on him in truth.
He fulfills the desires
of those who fear him;
he hears their cry
and saves them.

Psalm 145:18-19

Calvin Coolidge said, "People criticize me for harping on the obvious. Yet, if all the folks in the United States would do the few simple things they know they ought to do, most of our big problems would take care of themselves." For the Christian who wants to grow, the most basic of all activities is prayer. Although most Christians would agree with this statement, as the frustrated Coolidge pointed out, most of us don't do the things we ought to do.

One praying mantis was overheard saying to another, "I can't help it—I just don't feel like praying!" It is so easy to let our personal time of communication with God slip by in favor of other activities.

We need to look to the life of Jesus for our foremost

example in prayer. "Very early in the morning, while it was still dark, Jesus got up, left the house and went off to a solitary place, where he prayed" (Mark 1:35). It is remarkable that Jesus prayed at all. After all, He was God. And yet He had a need to communicate with His Father, to develop a close working relationship.

While confronting the Pharisees, Jesus said that He didn't do anything unless He saw the Father doing it (John 5:19). He was available to be shown by the Father because He was communicating with the Father on a regular basis. If we want to walk with God, we need to get to know God. Certainly the best way to get to know God is to spend time with Him and talk with Him.

There are four foundation stones in the Christian life. They are the "four talks." *Talk to* is prayer; *talk back* is God speaking back to us through the Bible; *talk with* is fellowship with believers; and *talk about* is witnessing.

We Christians must be actively involved in the art of communication with our heavenly Father, "rooted and built up in him, strengthened in the faith as [we] were taught" (Colossians 2:7). There is no other way to develop a life of faith, which is the only life pleasing to Him. If you do these four talks, your spiritual life will be solid. You will grow. You will mature.

✦ ✦ ✦

In order to be effective in prayer we must believe that it works. If we don't believe that prayer actually works, then we will probably invest almost all our time in something else.

We should, according to the axiom, talk to God about men and then talk to men about God. Our prayers should always precede our walk. We are sometimes faced with the decision either to go or to stay and pray. "Would it do more good if I spend this thirty minutes praying or if I make a few phone calls?" "Should I spend this morning's devotional time in prayer or in having coffee with that friend?" The answer is usually to pray. Oswald Chambers said, "Prayer does not fit us for the greater works; prayer *is* the greater work."

Prayer should never be taken to the extreme as an excuse for disobedience. When Scripture clearly outlines a mode of behavior, it is not necessary to pray about it for an extended period of time; it is time to obey. We do not need to pray about giving; we need to pray about where to give, and then we need to give. We do not need to pray about whether or not to witness; we simply need to open our mouths and speak.

On one Christian college campus the chaplain noticed two students standing in the parking lot praying one Sunday morning. He asked them what they were doing and they told him they were waiting for God to tell them which church bus to take. He looked around and all but one bus was pulling out of the parking lot. "Take that one," he said. They thanked him joyfully and climbed on the bus, sure that God had used him to direct them to the perfect service.

Many a church business meeting has been brought to a close just short of really solving problems by someone who, frightened by the intensity of emotions, made the suggestion to stop and pray. Sometimes a difficult situation goes unresolved because people would rather pray, letting God handle it, than obey Scripture by confronting the reality as commanded in Matthew 5:23-24.

We should believe that prayer works because *it is our God-given opportunity.* God can relate to our needs as we express them. "Therefore, since we have a great high priest who has gone through the heavens, Jesus the Son of God, let us hold firmly to the faith we profess. For we do not have a high priest who is unable to sympathize with our weaknesses, but we have one who has been tempted in every way, just as we are —yet was without sin" (Hebrews 4:14-15). Jesus understands. It is easy to talk to someone who understands. That's why we should never hesitate to pray. It's that simple. There is nothing that we can talk to Jesus about that He hasn't gone through in some fashion.

"Let us then approach the throne of grace with confidence, so that we may receive mercy and find grace to help us in our time of need" (Hebrews 4:16). Because we know that Jesus is our merciful and faithful High Priest, we can enter God's presence at any time.

The Forty-second Psalm gives us insight into this privilege. It tells of encouragement for a traveling pilgrim, a song for the road. This pilgrim was in exile. He longed to be in Jerusalem because the temple was the only place where he could truly worship. He cried out to God, "As the deer pants for streams of water, so my soul pants for you, O God." He thirsted for God from the innermost part of his being. And yet he felt detached from Him.

Now, because Jesus Christ is the merciful and faithful High Priest, we can enter into the Holy of Holies, the very presence of God. We need not feel estranged from Him. We can be in His presence whenever we want to be with Him. Why? Because of Jesus. Anytime, anywhere, we can talk to God. It's an opportunity that we can't afford to pass up.

✦ ✦ ✦

Another positive aspect of opportunity in prayer is *praying in the name of Jesus*. We Christians are in the habit of

punctuating our prayers with the name of our Savior.
What prayer would be considered orthodox unless closed
"in the name of Jesus"? We give it little thought, and we
fail to understand its significance. For many, praying in
the name of Jesus is just a formula to give the prayer the
seal of approval and to make sure it is answered. But God
is so gracious that He probably doesn't count our superficial understanding against us. Even so, we need to understand why we should pray in the name of Jesus.

What does it mean to pray in the name of Jesus? This
question consumed my thinking during a week when I
was preparing a message in the section of the Upper
Room discourse in which Jesus told His disciples twice, "I
will do whatever you ask in my name" (John 14:13-14). Why
was this important? Was it simply an acknowledgment of
the Son of God's place of honor in our daily prayers? Then
it hit me.

Earlier that week my son had burst into the house
with a ragtag delegation from the neighborhood. With
several boys standing behind him, all looking appropriately
hungry, my son requested cinnamon jawbreakers for all.
At first I hesitated. This would mean a depletion of my
private stock. Then my son put me in a bind: "Dad, I
promised these guys that you would give them candy." He
had me. I didn't want him to look bad, so I took down my
candy sack and placed a shiny red ball in each out-
stretched hand.

I had given each boy candy in Kris's name. They
didn't get what was mine because of my good nature or
my relationship with them; they received candy based on
my relationship with my son. I wanted him to be happy
and have a good relationship with his friends; I wanted
him to look good in the eyes of his peers.

Although the Father doesn't answer our prayers simply

to make Jesus look good, there is a parallel here. Praying in the name of Jesus is requesting from the Father based on *Jesus'* relationship with the Father, not ours. Praying in the name of Jesus is admitting that without the special relationship of Father and Son our prayers would be worthless. Our rights in prayer are based on Christ's work, Christ's obedience, Christ's pleasing of His Father, and our acknowledgment that a mediator is needed for the bridging of man's relationship with a holy God.

The primary reason a Christian does something is because it has a basis in truth. The theological point just discussed must remain the foundation for invoking Jesus' name in prayer. There is, however, another dimension concerning praying in Jesus' name that deserves our attention. All of us have bad days: We oversleep and miss our prayer time, overeat and ruin our diet, put off some work and feel guilty, pass up two choice witnessing opportunities, quarrel with our mate, and scream at the kids. In order to make sure the day is not a total loss, we kneel beside the bed and try to get right with God before we fall into bed.

> "Dear Lord,
>
> I know You're probably not listening—not that You should, seeing the day I've had. Lord, please forgive me. I'm not going to ask You for anything because we both know I don't deserve it. If I have a better day tomorrow, I'll give You my requests. I have a lot of them, but I'm saving them for one of my 'good days.' Hopefully I will see You tomorrow.
>
> In Jesus' name. Amen."

Sound familiar? Most of us have at least felt this prayer, even if we weren't bold enough to verbalize it.

Conversely, all of us have good days, when it seems as though the Holy Spirit writes the script and we play it perfectly. The prayer time, diet, work, and family relationships are right. We even take that opportunity to share the faith, which is truly the icing on the cake. It's the kind of day that makes life worthwhile. After such a day it's a pleasure to boldy approach the throne of grace.

> "Dear Lord,
>   Thank You for such a great day. Your fingerprints were all over it. I know You like faith; it's the only thing that pleases You. So now, with the knowledge that nothing is impossible with You, I believe You for the following: [a long list follows, beginning with the salvation of the world and closing with a special request for a new underground sprinkling system].
>   In the great and mighty name of Jesus. Amen."

While I admit that these prayers are tongue in cheek, they represent how we often feel and pray. Even though we say we are praying in the name of Jesus when we utter these prayers, we are doing nothing of the kind. When we pray a puny prayer after a day of defeat, we are not praying in the name of Jesus; we are praying based on *our performance*. When we storm the throne of grace with overconfidence after a great day, we are not praying in the name of Jesus; we are praying based on *our performance*. The posture of our praying in these two cases is based on how we are doing rather than on what Christ has done. We are approaching the Father as though Jesus had done nothing.

The Father doesn't ignore me because of a bad performance or hear me because of a good one. The *only* reason the Father hears me is because of Jesus. This is the message of grace: that our relationship with the Father is based on the relationship between the Father and the Son, not on our own deeds or "rights."

The next time you catch yourself hesitating to pray because of a bad performance or rushing audaciously to the throne because of a good one, stop and remind yourself what it really means to pray in the name of Jesus.

✦ ✦ ✦

We should also believe that prayer works because *it has tremendous benefits.* God Himself promised us, "Call to me and I will answer you and tell you great and unsearchable things you do not know" (Jeremiah 33:3). Our God "is able to do immeasurably more than all we ask or imagine" (Ephesians 3:20). If we simply ask Him, He will do things within us that we haven't even dreamed about. God wants to do marvelous things among us, but first we must pray.

There is a seemingly negative side to God's activity. He may give us difficult circumstances in our lives that we do not anticipate in order to develop our character (James 1:2-4, Romans 5:3-4). In the midst of hard times, we can find comfort in knowing that there will eventually be relief. David said, "I sought the Lord, and he answered me; he delivered me from all my fears" (Psalm 34:4). William Temple, a great writer and theologian, said, "When my praying stops, my coincidences stop."

✦ ✦ ✦

In order to be effective in prayer we must understand it. One important dimension of prayer is *confession.* Proverbs 28:13 warns against hiding our sins from God: "He who conceals his sins does not prosper, but whoever confesses and renounces them finds mercy." We need to openly admit to God that we are sinners and that we have committed specific sins.

"If we confess our sins, [God] is faithful and just and will forgive us our sins" (1 John 1:9).

We need to be honest with God concerning our failings and needs. We gain a strong motivation to confess when we recognize that God does not hear our prayers when we "cherish sin" in our hearts (Psalm 66:18). God chooses not to respond to someone who clings to sin.

What about unknown personal sin? Psalm 19:12 clears the fog on this issue: "Who can discern his [own] errors? Forgive my hidden faults." If we ask God, He will not only cleanse us of those sins the Holy Spirit brings to our attention but He will also cleanse us of even the hidden faults. Can you imagine how depressing it would be if the Holy Spirit brought all our sins to our attention at once? I like just a little bit at a time, and the promise that He is taking care of the unrevealed.

Prayer should also include the dimension of *praise* (Hebrews 13:15). Our ineptitude in praising God is a weak cord in much of evangelicalism. We lose something when we fail to release our emotions to God for fear that people will think we are fanatical or unbalanced. "Through Jesus, therefore, let us continually offer to God a sacrifice of praise—the fruit of lips that confess his name" (Hebrews 13:15). This means specifically verbal praise to God. It is a sacrifice of our words, a sweet aroma to God.

When you start your prayer time to God, sing a few songs to Him. He won't even mind if it's a little off-key. I often sing when I'm alone with God. I have a few favorite songs I consider very worshipful, and they enhance the enjoyment of my praise time with God.

Another part of prayer is *thanksgiving*. Paul said, "Sing

and make music in your heart to the Lord, always giving thanks to God the Father for everything, in the name of our Lord Jesus Christ" (Ephesians 5:19-20). Always give thanks to God. Have a thankful attitude. This is evidence of being Spirit-filled. Not that we should always have a Pollyanna kind of happiness; but we are called to be thankful even for the bad things that are happening in our lives. We thank God for them by faith.

Matthew 21:22 states that *faith* is a necessary condition of prayer. The Gospels clearly teach that faith is essential for the subsequent response from God. However, there are other factors involved. If I draw a line down the center of a paper and list in the left column all the verses in the Bible that say faith is all that is necessary for answered prayer, and if on the right I list those verses that attach a condition such as a commandment-keeping or yielding to God, the faith-only column would be much longer than the conditional column. Both lists are valid; there are simply conditions to prayer that are integrally related to faith.

One of the conditions of prayer is remaining in Christ (John 15:7). This means that we are making progress toward what God wants, that we are being established in His Word and in prayer, that we are in fellowship with other believers, and that we are reaching out to others. These activities form a solid foundation for growth.

We are also told to *ask* when we pray (John 16:24). Often we don't receive from God because we just don't ask. One summer I was raising financial support for my travel and training expenses for a missionary organization. I went to see a supporter and asked him if he could help me. He said, "What do you need?" I said that I needed five hundred dollars. He got out his checkbook, laid it on the top of the car in the drizzling rain, and wrote out a check for five hundred dollars. Then he said, knowing the expenses were far greater than that, "Do you need anything else?"

I said, "Well . . . yes."

"Come on, you have not because you ask not. What do you really need?"

"Another one thousand dollars."

"Okay." He wrote me another check for one thousand dollars and said, "Don't be afraid to ask."

Another condition is that we pray *according to God's will*. "This is the assurance we have in approaching God: that if we ask anything according to his will, he hears us" (1 John 5:14). As we spiritually mature, there will be a smaller and smaller discrepancy between His will and our understanding of His will. We know many things about God's will from the commandments in Scripture. For example, we know that we are to tell others about Him. Therefore, if we pray in faith for opportunities to witness, we can be assured that He will bring us in contact with someone who needs to hear. God will give us the power to pray and all the strength we need to obey Him.

+ + +

In order to be effective in prayer we must know how to pray. We should set a time and a place, and make a commitment to prayer. Most of us won't be very effective at prayer if we have a haphazard plan, just fitting it in whenever we have a free moment. Those moments have a way of disintegrating into the busy rush of our days.

I believe the best time for prayer is *in the morning*. If we wait until the end of the day, we are often tired and unable to put our best into it. I tried the end-of-the-day method and fell asleep a few times. David said to God, "Morning by morning, O Lord, you hear my voice; morning by morning I lay my requests before you and wait in expectation" (Psalm 5:3). We are to give God the first fruits of our lives. Think of morning prayer as giving God the first fruits of your day. The principle found from Genesis to Revelation is the importance of giving God from off the top, giving Him the best.

Colossians 4:2 refers to the value of *alertness* as we pray. Half-hearted praying is not up to God's standard. Pray out loud. Because there is no audible feedback from God, it is especially easy to lose concentration in silent prayer. So if you speak to God aloud, you can stay more alert.

After you have established a time and place and committed yourself to the task of prayer, *you need a plan.* There are several books that can help you. One is called *Seven Minutes With God,* a pamphlet by NavPress. Another is *Appointment With God,* also by NavPress.

But please don't allow devotional guides to become the staple of your devotional life. There is no substitute for the Bible because it is the only book you can read that is supernatural. Let God speak to you directly through His Word, and keep a journal of your insights.

Next, *make a prayer list.* Here are some suggestions: pray for your family, nonChristians, Christians, your pastor, missionaries, church workers, those who oppose you, government authorities, and personal needs. I suggest you spend part of your prayer time using the list and then some free flow. It is also important to spend some time listening to God. I'm not talking about mysticism, but just sitting quietly before the God who said, "Be still, and know that I am God" (Psalm 46:10).

In order to keep my devotional time fresh and to avoid repetition, I pray for different things on different days. Each day of the week has its own category, such as missionaries on Monday, the Church on Tuesday, etc. Every now and then I revise and rotate the prayer needs.

It is a good idea to *record the answers to prayer.* Compile a daily journal of the working of God in your life. Whenever you feel down and you think that your prayers aren't getting any higher than the ceiling, just look through the journal and remember what God has taught you through His Word and what significant answers to prayer you have received.

If you miss your devotional time, don't allow Satan to put you on a guilt trip and discourage you from doing it the next time. This is very important. Satan wants us to feel guilty and give up. But God wants us to forego the guilt and get started again the next day.

The buddy system is a good method to keep you on track. Find a friend to pray with, even if it is just for a couple of times a week. Share with this friend what God has been teaching you. Make plans to read a particular book of the Bible together; then discuss it whenever you get together. This is a mutual encouragement and the most positive kind of accountability.

Prayer is the gymnasium of the soul. It takes a real effort. Somedays I don't feel like exercising, but I do it anyhow. And when I am consistent, I feel stronger. I can go upstairs without huffing and puffing, and I can see results. A person who is faithful in prayer thinks progressively more in tune with God's Word and is progressively more open to the leading of God's Spirit.

E.M. Bounds wrote, "The men who have most fully illustrated Christ in their character and have most powerfully affected the world for Him, have been men that have spent so much time with God as to make it a notable feature in their lives. To be little with God is to be little for God."

EPILOGUE

*How great are
your works, O Lord,
how profound your
thoughts!*

Psalm 92:5

The mind is the command center that directly affects the body and soul. As far as spiritual growth is concerned, right *thinking* logically precedes right *being* and right *action.*

Our God is the One who "forms the mountains, creates the wind, and reveals his thoughts to man" (Amos 4:13). The only right thinking is *God's* thinking. He has revealed His thoughts to us in His Word, the Bible.

All true followers of Jesus want to experience spiritual growth. But maturity is not an automatic thing. We need to engage our minds if we want to change for the better. God will provide the rest.

As we learn, through the Spirit's guidance, how to

read God's Word (thereby reading God's mind), we can mature in our understanding of the spiritual realm. In some cases we encounter a "first learning" of spiritual principles. In other cases we need to unlearn and then relearn.

Here are three principles to apply in your quest toward greater spiritual maturity: (1) Fill your mind with God's thoughts by reading Scripture. By doing so, your mind will inevitably be transformed, renewed, fulfilled. As you see life through the eyes of God, you will be able to maintain a steady course throughout your spiritual life. (2) Don't wait for spiritual growth to happen to you; actively pursue it! Step out in obedience, emphasizing the basics of the Word, prayer, fellowship, and witnessing. (3) Get the right kind of experience with the right kind of people. Find people of kindred spirit who also want to pursue the adventure of spiritual growth.

Don't waste the precious gift of life. Make your life count. If right thinking is not a part of your armor, the insidious propaganda of the world will eventually conform you to its image. But the call of Christ to all His followers is to fulfill your Spirit-engendered destiny. "For those God foreknew he also predestined to be conformed to the likeness of his Son, that he might be the firstborn among many brothers" (Romans 8:29).

ACKNOWLEDGMENTS

I want to express my gratitude to Kathy Yanni, whose encouragement has stimulated me to write; to Jon Stine, whose insightful editing has enhanced the ministry of my books; and to Don Simpson, whose creative ideas have expanded my thinking.